18 DAYS
BRAIN TRAINING
1/3

Start Your Workout!

www.alexanderhalm.de

18 DAYS BRAIN TRAINING 1/3

Start Your Workout!

Alexander Halm

First published 2020

Copyright © 2020 by A. Halm

ISBN 9798667240099

Independently published

www.alexanderhalm.de

Place of publication: Alexander Halm - Schweinsdorf 64 - 91616 Neusitz

Please visit the website www.alexanderhalm.de for further contact information.

**"Your brain is like a muscle.
If you train it, it stays strong.**
Without practice, decay begins."

A. Halm

CONTENTS

A FEW SECONDS THAT CAN CHANGE YOUR PERFORMANCE!

"Start every day with a smile
and every training with relaxation!"

A foreword should point out the most important things and lead you to the topic. So let's do it: with this series of books you have the opportunity to train your brain in certain areas. This can help you at school, at work, in everyday life and keep your brain fit even in old age.

But before you start, always remember:
"Sometimes things go faster if you take your time."

RELAX FOR 30 SECONDS

Do this at the beginning of each unit:

1. Close your eyes and count slowly to 10.

2. Take three deep breaths in and out.

3. Stretch both arms up in the winning pose, raise your head and say: "I'm great, I can do it!"

4. Open your eyes again and start the exercise.

HOW TO USE THIS BOOK

READ THIS BEFORE YOU START!

I would like to give you some useful tips.

This book series consists of three volumes of increasing difficulty. For optimal exercise success, you should work on all three in succession:

> **Volume 1: Start Your Workout!**
> **Volume 2: Enter the Next Level!**
> **Volume 3: Enduring Brainpower!**

Each book has 18 units, one per day. The individual units can be processed in a relatively short time. If you feel good, you can also work on several units per day. You will see - IT`S FUN!

Since you want to train your brain in general and don't want to memorize anything for a long period of time, it doesn't really matter when and where you do it. You should only be able to concentrate well and not be distracted. So you can train anytime, anywhere.

In order to achieve the best possible training effect, test subjects were confronted with various types of tasks and sequences over a longer period of time. This book series was created after evaluating the test results, including didactic considerations.

The exercises are disigned to train your brain effectively in certain areas without wasting your time! Therefore unnecessary games were avoided. Brain training is like doing sports. To train perfectly, you have to do the same exercises over and over again. Only then you you have the chance to get better after a while.

HOW TO USE THIS BOOK

The order of the tasks is the same for all days:

1. WARM UP! (math and logic skills)
To warm up, do some simple math and decipher a given code.

2. WORDS AND LETTERS (reading skills)
You focus on the task and practice intuitively recognizing strings in a large collection of characters.

3. CALCULATE (math)
Full concentration! Do the math as fast as you can and try, if possible, to intuitively recognize the solution.

4. FIND THE NUMBERS! (optical recognition - memorizing)
Finally, you practice recognizing given numbers of different sizes as quickly as possible in a field of numbers. Additionally you can show how good your memory is.

With this mix of simple but effective exercises, you can not only improve your performance, but also have a lot of fun!

It makes sense to complete all of the tasks in the entire unit first before comparing your results. This procedure increases concentration and takes less time.

You learn best when it's fun!

So always remember: you are not a computer! In order to train your brain, not all solutions have to be 100% correct. Just try to do your best.

HOW TO USE THIS BOOK

DECIPHERING TASKS

In each unit you will find a decryption task. To make it easy to get started with this volume, it is a simple "Caesar encryption". The name comes from the famous Roman emperor.

The encryption works according to the following principle:

The sender of the message encrypts his text by shifting each letter by a certain number (offset) in one direction (here to the left). The spaces are also considered here as characters!

And this is how YOU decrypt the given code:

To get the original text, you have to move each letter to the right by the specified number of characters (offset). **Use the alphabet printed below the task.** Important: You also have to decipher the spaces, because these will then become letters!

EXAMPLE

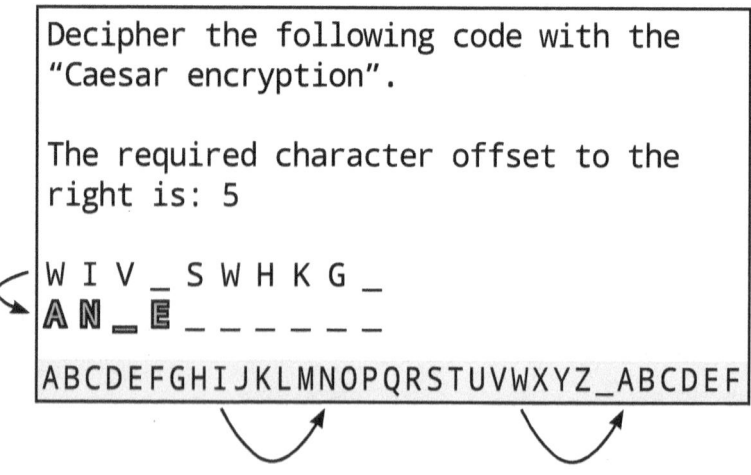

Decipher the following code with the "Caesar encryption".

The required character offset to the right is: 5

W I V _ S W H K G _
A N _ E _ _ _ _ _ _

ABCDEFGHIJKLMNOPQRSTUVWXYZ_ABCDEF

12

HOW TO USE THIS BOOK

Solution for the example:

All code letters must be shifted to the right with an offset of 5 characters using the alphabet:

```
W  +  5  =  A
I  +  5  =  N
V  +  5  =  _
_  +  5  =  E
S  +  5  =  X
W  +  5  =  A
H  +  5  =  M
K  +  5  =  P
G  +  5  =  L
_  +  5  =  E
```

I wish you great success in your daily training!

And now ... let's get started!

day 1

CHECKING YOUR CALCULATION RESULTS IS EASY!

Just turn over the page!

The solutions for the math tasks can always be found on the edge of the pages before and after.

Example:
The solutions for page 16 are on page 18.
The solutions for page 21 are on page 19.

WARM UP!

Do the whole day's session first before checking your results.

3 + 8 = _____	6 • 3 = _____
8 + 2 = _____	12 + 13 = _____
7 + 9 = _____	21 - 18 = _____
3 + 10 = _____	9 • 4 = _____
9 + 5 = _____	13 - 8 = _____
3 • 3 = _____	29 - 14 = _____
12 + 7 = _____	4 + 6 = _____
3 • 6 = _____	11 + 16 = _____
13 - 3 = _____	3 • 7 = _____
7 + 12 = _____	5 • 6 = _____
14 - 14 = _____	18 - 5 = _____
3 + 7 = _____	17 + 10 = _____
15 - 8 = _____	30 - 6 = _____
2 • 9 = _____	5 • 5 = _____
14 - 13 = _____	9 • 2 = _____
2 • 4 = _____	14 + 5 = _____
14 - 3 = _____	8 + 19 = _____
11 + 9 = _____	7 + 15 = _____
10 + 6 = _____	4 • 10 = _____
3 • 5 = _____	13 + 8 = _____

For an introduction, see pages 12 and 13.

Decipher the following code with the "Caesar encryption".

The required character offset to the right is: 4

P D A W N K I X J

_ _ _ _ _ _ _ _ _

Copy the decrypted text on page 197.

ABCDEFGHIJKLMNOPQRSTUVWXYZ_ABCDEF

Memorize this picture and all of its details as best as you can to make a sketch of it later.

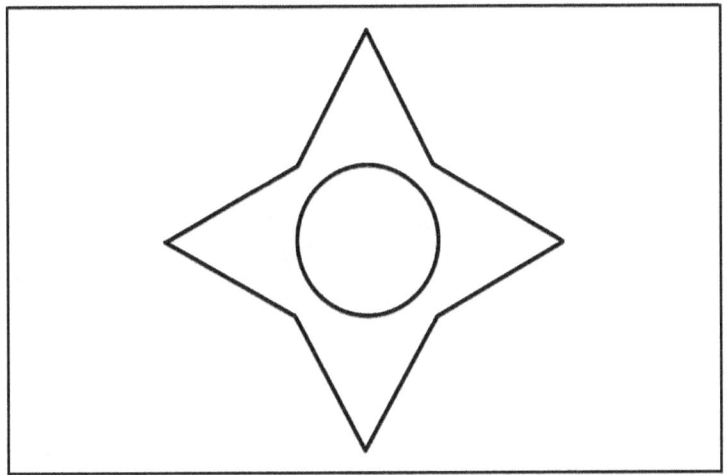

WORDS AND LETTERS

Mark and count the words and letters line by line. Do it only once!

<-- 16

11	18
10	25
16	3
13	36
14	5
9	15
19	10
18	27
10	21
19	30

Mark and count: V

```
XXXXXXXXVXXXXXXXXXXXXXXXXXXXXXXXXVX
XXXXXXXXXXXXXXXXXXXXXXXXXXXXXXXXXXX
XXXXXXXXXXXXXXXXXXXXXXXXXXXXXXXXXXX
XXXXXXXXXXXXXXXXXXXXXXXXXXXXXXXXXXX
XXXXXXXXXXXXXXXXXXXXXXXXXXXXMALXVXXXV
XXXXXVXXXXXXXXXXXXXXXXXVXXXXXXXXVXX
XXXXXXXXXXXXXXVXXXXXXXXXXXXXXXXXXXV
XXXXXXXXXXXVXXXVXXXXXXXXXXXXXXXXXXX
XXXXXXXXXXXXXXXXXXXXXXXXXXXXXXXXXXX
XXXXXVXXXXXXXXXVXXXXXXXVXXXVXXXXXVX
XXXXXXXXXXXXXXXXXXVXXXXXXXXXXVXXXX
VXXXXXXXXXXXXXXXXXXXXXXXXXXXXXXXXXX
XXXXXXXXXXVXXXXXXXXXXVXXXXXXXXXXXV
```

Mark and count: LIMA

0	13
10	27
7	24
18	25
1	18
8	19
11	27
20	22
16	40
15	21

```
LIMAAIIMAIMMAIMMLIMMILLIMALMILLAMAL
ILAMAMAMAIAIAMAMLIALAALILIMAAMLAAAM
ILLMIIALLALIMALLILALIIILMMLMAIMLMAA
LILIIIALILIMALLIMMMMAAIMLLMMLMIIAAI
IMALILLAAMMILILLIMALLMIALIIAMAIIALA
LMIMIIIAILAAALMAMAMAMIAAMIMLILLALIL
AMLALIAMLIMALIMALIIMLMLLIMAMLMMLAML
LLMMIIAILIAMLMALLAALIMALIMAIIMMLIMM
AAALAIIIILLIMAMAMAAMMMMLLMIMMAMAMIM
AMIMILLLALIALLAIILLLLMIAIIMMMAAIIMA
AIAILMLLAAAMMMAIIMMILIMAAAAALIMAAML
IIIMMIALIMAMAIMAAMIIILLAAMLIMILLIAL
ALIMAAAIAMMIIIMILLMILIALMAALIMMAMIM
```

18

Decrypted original text from the previous page:
THE ROMAN

21 -->

Mark and count: SYBILLE

10	16
70	1
28	1
72	30
28	30
13	16
18	11
54	3
37	15
10	32
4	24
42	11
17	28
34	21
23	12
21	29
50	1
27	26
29	25
24	16

```
JPXGDSYBILLEKJEUOSYVNRKDDEQXNFPBNYZ
ALZJTKJIAXRSXONMUBJNAGHUCHGNWUGSCLE
FSYBILLEFKISYBILLERSONISYBILLEADVSY
UTIVIKKEQDIGTHFDHPOOQDMALPHESYBILLE
VLZOWJIAFVGXSYBILLEHTKYISFSYBILLEYC
VTDLHIHSSSYBILLESYBILLERLDAOZHXUFPW
SYBILLELKMYQRQKZRLUTSYBILLERBVJFVJP
MRZZSYBILLEWAORSLRSKULSYBILLELRFQFG
CIJJGJFRVTNGRZHUHSQQSMOTJGLUVFEWQKW
WMVKGRZLAMFXLCQBPIRILFGMRXRKZZRYVTQ
KLSYBILLEUTVUHWSYBILLEKBIUBPGSWEABQ
ZSCSJAFFRTFAMPMOLEALUEMGZHIRVHCVUKZ
VLNOKNIGSYBILLEHESWSYBILLEPIRNCNPRK
KWGGJQZCULNPZJCIDIBREGCPRHGAKRSEQBW
XBGJRKOSYBILLESYBILLEOUBELPRAYGQRWT
GWTSYBILLEGSQIHAKISSYBILLETEUQENFBC
YSYBILLETYXEADSYBILLEKARCSDKDBGMIOH
UOGSSYBILLEERCGXFBMWYSYBILLEFKANYZQ
BGSUTTFQDAXPTNXJXUCNJYIRMPEUXJSEASE
SYBILLEHKLSKOPPMWSYBILLEKYYSYBILLEH
EUSLMXEXWSYBILLESYBILLEWUAZZNXAWAPF
EPOOWKAXBCHUSYBILLEWSYBILLEYYARIPMR
MWUWXJYLDDOBTBSJCLTVNWSYBILLESACOWU
OSMVDPZLSESYBILLEFPSYBILLEICBKVNEQK
ZZDASYBILLEDKBVLJXDODQFDSNCSYBILLEG
RSYBILLELDGAPSYBILLEZTPFKNBBVEJIUGD
PLUBGTVHMGOEERVZCUEWLYSMHDVSQFFIMGN
DIICSWSYBILLEFLZVUJXTSYBILLERPWKKQB
ZIFGFAYIMZFMIDRSYBILLESYBILLEKILFPO
```

Are you sure? See page 194!

CALCULATE

15 - 9 = _____	21 - 10 = _____
10 + 7 = _____	4 • 4 = _____
6 • 2 = _____	8 + 14 = _____
6 • 3 = _____	5 + 23 = _____
6 - 6 = _____	14 + 14 = _____
3 + 10 = _____	16 + 8 = _____
4 • 5 = _____	5 + 12 = _____
2 + 13 = _____	14 + 16 = _____
3 • 6 = _____	4 • 9 = _____
2 • 3 = _____	17 + 13 = _____
2 + 8 = _____	14 - 3 = _____
2 • 6 = _____	22 - 5 = _____
13 - 8 = _____	13 + 5 = _____
5 + 2 = _____	4 + 21 = _____
7 + 10 = _____	13 + 9 = _____
8 • 3 = _____	7 + 4 = _____
6 + 3 = _____	13 - 11 = _____
2 • 9 = _____	7 • 4 = _____
5 • 4 = _____	20 - 19 = _____
3 • 3 = _____	8 • 5 = _____

$5 \cdot 2 =$ _____	$2 \cdot 8 =$ _____
$7 \cdot 10 =$ _____	$30 - 29 =$ _____
$21 + 7 =$ _____	$8 - 7 =$ _____
$8 \cdot 9 =$ _____	$26 + 4 =$ _____
$4 \cdot 7 =$ _____	$12 + 18 =$ _____
$31 - 18 =$ _____	$6 + 10 =$ _____
$27 - 9 =$ _____	$30 - 19 =$ _____
$9 \cdot 6 =$ _____	$24 - 21 =$ _____
$28 + 9 =$ _____	$5 \cdot 3 =$ _____
$28 - 18 =$ _____	$4 \cdot 8 =$ _____
$2 \cdot 2 =$ _____	$9 + 15 =$ _____
$26 + 16 =$ _____	$18 - 7 =$ _____
$33 - 16 =$ _____	$4 + 24 =$ _____
$23 + 11 =$ _____	$29 - 8 =$ _____
$30 - 7 =$ _____	$3 \cdot 4 =$ _____
$14 + 7 =$ _____	$18 + 11 =$ _____
$5 \cdot 10 =$ _____	$29 - 28 =$ _____
$9 \cdot 3 =$ _____	$21 + 5 =$ _____
$44 - 15 =$ _____	$9 + 16 =$ _____
$50 - 26 =$ _____	$11 + 5 =$ _____

FIND THE NUMBERS

Mark and count the numbers line by line. Do it only once!

<-- 20

6	11
17	16
12	22
18	28
0	28
13	24
20	17
15	30
18	36
6	30
10	11
12	17
5	18
7	25
17	22
24	11
9	2
18	28
20	1
9	40

Mark and count: 8

```
0 5 5 2 8 9 4 8 4 0 5 1 5 3 1 5 2 5
9 8 7 5 8 4 8 3 7 8 9 7 1 1 6 8 4 9
2 7 1 4 5 3 4 1 6 0 9 6 6 9 4 6 3 5
9 3 8 0 2 9 0 4 9 6 6 0 7 6 9 6 5 4
4 1 1 2 9 2 0 5 0 4 4 0 7 6 9 4 3 6
5 1 8 4 8 6 6 4 9 8 2 8 9 3 4 6 1 7
2 1 0 4 1 1 9 8 3 6 2 9 9 9 7 0 8 3
3 3 0 0 1 7 7 3 1 6 1 1 0 4 9 5 9 4
0 9 3 8 4 2 9 0 5 4 0 2 7 8 4 6 7 4
6 0 3 8 0 1 4 8 5 7 4 6 0 1 4 2 5 9
7 0 9 0 0 9 6 7 0 8 4 1 5 0 2 4 3 6
2 0 6 8 9 4 4 9 1 6 6 4 7 4 7 6 5 1
9 5 8 0 9 6 9 8 1 1 7 7 0 3 5 5 7 8
```

Mark and count: 20

```
61 34 19 17 83 85 85 48 18 65 20 30
48 20 52 78 20 52 41 90 67 91 13 20
67 29 26 89 74 21 83 55 72 51 24 62
24 38 74 20 22 62 90 39 34 26 14 40
78 93 63 52 81 20 46 87 57 17 22 20
94 52 31 17 32 71 20 93 67 33 16 64
75 84 27 10 11 34 61 22 83 42 83 64
86 91 65 58 84 25 30 84 54 76 16 66
31 54 35 20 20 54 88 41 58 72 35 17
47 39 45 51 20 83 63 98 17 81 60 45
59 87 53 95 24 80 18 20 20 17 21 65
53 17 58 59 95 18 10 97 31 47 20 91
79 47 50 30 23 66 22 12 59 78 10 88
```

Are you sure? See page 195!

Now make a simple sketch of the memorized picture
with as many details as possible:

TRY TO REMEMBER!

What should you find?

- City: _____
- Name: _____
- Decrypted text: _____

day 2

WARM UP!

12 - 2 = _____	8 + 10 = _____
8 • 2 = _____	26 - 15 = _____
14 + 3 = _____	19 + 7 = _____
3 • 3 = _____	27 - 27 = _____
8 + 8 = _____	7 + 17 = _____
10 - 8 = _____	5 • 7 = _____
6 - 2 = _____	9 + 11 = _____
4 • 6 = _____	18 - 9 = _____
15 - 15 = _____	11 - 3 = _____
20 - 18 = _____	27 - 25 = _____
2 • 4 = _____	7 • 6 = _____
19 - 5 = _____	7 + 9 = _____
15 - 7 = _____	3 • 6 = _____
5 • 4 = _____	6 + 4 = _____
4 + 11 = _____	4 • 9 = _____
7 • 3 = _____	6 + 22 = _____
10 • 2 = _____	4 • 3 = _____
12 - 7 = _____	9 • 3 = _____
3 • 7 = _____	17 + 8 = _____
6 • 3 = _____	7 - 7 = _____

Decipher the following code with the "Caesar encryption".

The required character offset to the right is: 5

_ H K _ M J M V B W D P N

_ _ _ _ _ _ _ _ _ _ _ _ _ _

Copy the decrypted text on page 197.

ABCDEFGHIJKLMNOPQRSTUVWXYZ_ABCDEF

Memorize this picture and all of its details as best as you can to make a sketch of it later.

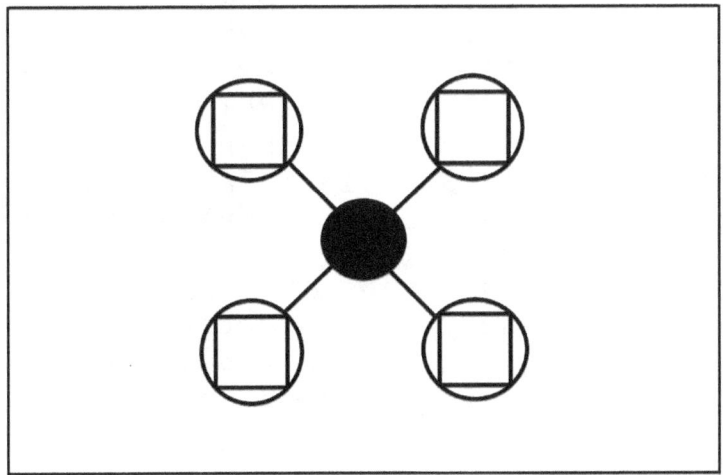

<-- 26

10	18
16	11
17	26
9	0
16	24
2	35
4	20
24	9
0	8
2	2
8	42
14	16
8	18
20	10
15	36
21	28
20	12
5	27
21	25
18	0

Mark and count: G

```
OOOOOOOOOOOOOOOOOOOOOOOOOOOOOOOOOOOOOO
OOOOOOOOOGOOOOOOOOOOOOGOOOOOOOOOOOO
OOOOOOOOOOOOOOOOOOOOOOOOOOOGOOOOOOOO
OOOOOOOOOOOOOOOOOOOOOOOOOOOOOOOOOOOO
OOOOOOOOOOGOOOOOGOOOOOOOOOOOOOOOO
OOOOOOOOOOOOOOOOOOOOGOOOOOOOGOOOOO
OOOOOOOOOOOOOOOOOOOOOOOGOOOOOOOOO
OOOOOOOOOOOOOOGOOOOOOOOOOGOOOOO
OOOOOOOOOGOOOGOOOOOOOOOOOOOOOOOOGOO
OOOOOOOOOOOOOOOOOOOOOOOOOOOOOOOO
OOOOOOOOOOOOOOOOOOOOOOOOOOOOOOO
OOOOOOOOOOOOOOOOOOOOOOOOOOOOOOO
OOOOGOOOOOOOOOOOOOOOOOOOOOOOOOO
```

Mark and count: PARIS

```
AAPPRIPRPPSSAIISAPAASAPSIRAIAAIIPIR
ARAPARRAPPIAIRASAPARISRRPRRSAAARRRA
PSPSPRIPRPAIAIRRSSPPPPPRIPSPARISISI
AASRRIRPPIIARPARISAPSIRRIIAPAPRARRR
RSARSSISPARISPISIPIISRRPRPRPRRSAAAI
RSPAPRSSAAIPASAIPSIPARISARRSPARISRS
AIAPPARISSPARISSIAAIARPPPRPARISASRS
IAIPARPAPRRRAPISIPIAIRPRAIIRAPARIS
PARISISSRAAPIIIPARSSIPRAIRAIRRPIPRI
IPRARIRSIPARISAAIPRISIIRPPASIPIRAPI
RSSPARISSSPIAAAIASASPIAIPIRSRAPAIAI
ISRAIISSPPASIIAISSIIRPSARPARISIRPSP
SIRIPAPIAARPIRIRPPARISRSRPAISAPPIAR
```

Decrypted original text from the previous page:
EMPEROR GAIUS

31 -->

Mark and count: VICTOR

34	3
16	9
6	26
53	9
18	18
34	18
29	18
60	8
30	11
24	20
59	6
1	20
20	36
4	0
4	10
34	27
27	13
31	28
38	6
37	2

```
RWLKZVICTORFBGDVLAZUBNDZWTIVMSIIEEV
SXGMVZWVICTORLWRVUFGXJNCGHVMFQEAPEZ
URCVHYACZYHWDKRWWXQOZHBOMEVICTORMWZ
RUSTVICTORINWKBFTAXESTPQZSJNZDPBSFC
ODRXLVJCLYHESEVICTORGIMZLPNFSELPFKV
QIDLJPDSZIUKQVICTORJBCXQHGDLOYEBNNF
QABZKUOGZZNEKJCASEDVICTORYQUZXNARKB
PNWVICTORZKZXOYTTRVICTORVICTORNXSXE
CFNVICTORXKJUUAGATNGOCCLNQBYMFMPYLR
DIZBDXVZMBIAYNVPVJVICTORXFVVICTORGQ
XEBHIVJEJCVICTORHOPWZRBZCCYLYVYCGGE
PQIFRHOHDYQAQBUIIMVICTORPZPWFOYGNPT
IYXPCROWGXFJUQEOGHUXYZYVICTORHNYBTX
SYVRQZEEOCPKWYVUKXPPWDERIVICTORKQZT
CXLBUNSNUFVHRUVICTORFKTVICTORVZLYRE
OCOKELNFOKMXNIBHEXONTXEFXURTXGVTAFX
VXQUOVZQWIVICTORMPRSZGIRHIYUOERUQFS
KLBACUMJHALGOKRTKJOLTAEPCMBRWEWUUAN
MBLFCBQLDEVICTORNSAYHLZZGVJDCOLBNEK
DKVNTRVICTORWEBUYMSGGICEYTFTQINOYVJ
LCKSGFORQHZFADOFIXNFZCXHOCLJVKCAHTQ
UXKTEBALTLKOPHEFGCFWVICTORSUCKTEPSK
EKLZZYJVICTORRYOSNVICTORVZMPPBXRQQA
IFKVICTORDFOVICTORBICAMMVNJCXBAFLHT
XXXXNYTDVICTORJXKYKWYWIPJRIJQHACADM
JHLVICTORKVICTORKQJVMHOWGDCZVICTORC
NCPOBXTZZUIWAEQEOVICTORZXSVICTORCTH
XKJVICTORXPWLGMESBVICTORCLZQMAOWWKS
KPGEGTGCKICWDXAMMZMDVICTORMRJDIXWZV
```

Are you sure? See page 194!

CALCULATE

8 - 6 = _____	15 - 9 = _____
4 • 3 = _____	7 • 3 = _____
2 + 11 = _____	18 - 12 = _____
14 - 11 = _____	24 - 5 = _____
6 - 5 = _____	28 - 26 = _____
15 - 8 = _____	4 • 9 = _____
18 - 2 = _____	13 - 10 = _____
5 + 14 = _____	19 - 14 = _____
9 • 2 = _____	4 • 4 = _____
4 - 2 = _____	21 + 6 = _____
4 • 6 = _____	8 + 21 = _____
2 • 7 = _____	7 + 6 = _____
5 • 4 = _____	8 + 6 = _____
4 • 5 = _____	16 - 10 = _____
20 - 6 = _____	4 • 2 = _____
5 • 3 = _____	5 + 21 = _____
6 • 3 = _____	8 + 15 = _____
15 - 7 = _____	13 + 17 = _____
6 • 2 = _____	18 + 7 = _____
13 + 5 = _____	4 + 20 = _____

Additional tasks - only for math lovers!

$17 + 17 =$ _____ $22 - 19 =$ _____

$50 - 34 =$ _____ $20 - 11 =$ _____

$3 \cdot 2 =$ _____ $30 - 4 =$ _____

$20 + 33 =$ _____ $23 - 14 =$ _____

$50 - 32 =$ _____ $30 - 12 =$ _____

$6 + 28 =$ _____ $6 \cdot 3 =$ _____

$37 - 8 =$ _____ $5 + 13 =$ _____

$6 \cdot 10 =$ _____ $17 - 9 =$ _____

$22 + 8 =$ _____ $20 - 9 =$ _____

$8 \cdot 3 =$ _____ $30 - 10 =$ _____

$24 + 35 =$ _____ $2 \cdot 3 =$ _____

$29 - 28 =$ _____ $4 \cdot 5 =$ _____

$41 - 21 =$ _____ $6 \cdot 6 =$ _____

$39 - 35 =$ _____ $14 - 14 =$ _____

$45 - 41 =$ _____ $2 \cdot 5 =$ _____

$10 + 24 =$ _____ $20 + 7 =$ _____

$3 \cdot 9 =$ _____ $25 - 12 =$ _____

$45 - 14 =$ _____ $7 \cdot 4 =$ _____

$29 + 9 =$ _____ $9 - 3 =$ _____

$8 + 29 =$ _____ $13 - 11 =$ _____

FIND THE NUMBERS!

<-- 30

2	6
12	21
13	6
3	19
1	2
7	36
16	3
19	5
18	16
2	27
24	29
14	13
20	14
20	6
14	8
15	26
18	23
8	30
12	25
18	24

Mark and count: 2

```
8 1 6 5 1 1 2 0 7 2 8 8 5 7 6 1 2 3
7 7 3 4 7 9 5 1 7 4 7 5 8 1 5 5 7 1
0 9 0 7 9 7 4 1 2 4 0 1 9 0 0 8 8 1
1 2 4 3 9 0 1 0 4 9 8 1 3 9 4 8 2 2
2 5 8 5 1 2 4 8 1 5 7 9 5 5 4 5 2 3
8 5 2 5 9 6 1 9 8 7 2 7 1 0 8 5 0 0
5 3 3 7 4 9 7 8 3 8 7 5 4 4 5 9 3 9
6 4 3 6 0 9 6 3 8 8 4 7 1 5 8 8 1 6
2 9 6 3 8 2 7 6 3 1 5 8 2 6 7 4 7 7
3 9 4 2 0 7 4 6 8 9 0 1 9 9 1 8 5 2
9 0 9 0 6 9 7 7 4 1 5 4 8 9 5 1 1 3
9 1 1 3 4 2 3 2 4 4 0 0 3 1 3 1 4 2
5 9 0 7 2 9 5 9 4 3 7 8 4 8 3 1 1 7
```

Mark and count: 41

```
14 40 58 19 59 15 43 82 70 67 87 41
27 19 89 50 99 43 23 13 73 48 17 46
33 85 40 47 30 88 75 47 17 64 82 82
27 65 41 22 83 69 81 70 41 32 83 95
55 83 71 80 88 85 95 40 40 77 49 98
41 41 56 41 77 56 54 81 41 82 59 92
54 95 23 53 59 21 68 42 61 47 41 96
32 46 49 76 82 21 35 29 26 11 35 81
39 39 53 41 44 93 41 12 73 79 15 67
61 37 43 89 38 82 74 10 14 49 58 99
25 53 15 12 82 61 56 63 41 64 17 41
20 90 52 75 39 43 73 41 47 92 16 46
61 75 46 96 41 31 72 41 36 89 57 92
```

Are you sure? See page 195!

Now make a simple sketch of the memorized picture
with as many details as possible:

TRY TO REMEMBER!

What should you find?

- City: _____
- Name: _____
- Decrypted text: _____

day 3

WARM UP!

8 • 2 = _____	11 + 13 = _____
4 + 14 = _____	13 + 17 = _____
4 + 12 = _____	23 - 18 = _____
14 - 11 = _____	22 - 17 = _____
10 + 8 = _____	4 • 8 = _____
4 + 10 = _____	8 + 21 = _____
3 + 6 = _____	29 - 7 = _____
2 • 2 = _____	19 + 8 = _____
18 - 13 = _____	13 + 16 = _____
3 • 7 = _____	28 - 15 = _____
3 • 8 = _____	6 + 8 = _____
16 + 2 = _____	3 • 2 = _____
3 + 16 = _____	9 + 11 = _____
5 • 4 = _____	7 + 13 = _____
2 + 6 = _____	9 • 3 = _____
7 + 8 = _____	7 • 3 = _____
13 - 10 = _____	25 - 11 = _____
14 - 10 = _____	12 - 8 = _____
8 + 12 = _____	13 + 8 = _____
10 • 2 = _____	18 + 12 = _____

Decipher the following code with the "Caesar encryption".

The required character offset to the right is: 3

G R I F R P X _ Y B P Y O

— — — — — — — — — — — — —

Copy the decrypted text on page 197.

ABCDEFGHIJKLMNOPQRSTUVWXYZ_ABCDEF

Memorize this picture and all of its details as best as you can to make a sketch of it later.

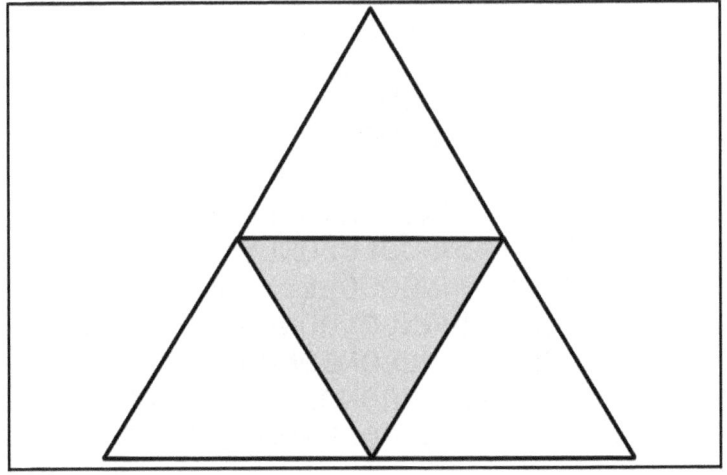

16 24
18 30
16 5
3 5
18 32
14 29
9 22
4 27
5 29
21 13
24 14
18 6
19 20
20 20
8 27
15 21
3 14
4 4
20 21
20 30

Mark and count: U

WWWWWWWWWWWWWWWWWWWWWWWWWUWWWWWWWW
WWWWWUWWWWWWWWWWWWWWWWWWWWWWWWWWWW
WWWWWWWWWWUWWWWWWWWWWWWWWWUWWWWWWW
WWWWWWWWWWWUWWWUWWWWWWWWWWWUWWUWUW
WWWWWWWWWWWWWWWWWWWWWWWWWWWWWWWWWW
WWWWWWWWWWWWWWWWWWWWWWWWWWWWWWWWWW
WWWWWUWWWWWWWWWWWWWWWWWWWWWWWWWWWW
WWWWWWWWWWWUWWWWWUWWWWWWWWWUWWWWWW
WWWWWWWWWWWWWWWWWWWWWWWWWWWWWWWWWW
WWWWWWWWWWWWWWWWWUUWWWWWWWWWWWWWWW
WWWWUWWWWWWWWWWWWWUWWWWWWWWWWWWWWW
WWWWWWWWWWWWWWWWWWWWWWWWWWWWWWWWWW
WUWWWWWWWWWWWWWWWWUWWWWWWWWWWWWWWW

Mark and count: LONDON

LONDONNONNNONNDLLNNNDONNLDOLOODDLNN
NOLOONNNONNLDOOLONDONODLOOLOLNLNOOO
LONDONLOLLLLONDONLONDONOLOOLOLDODOD
LONDONLNNNDOLNNDONONDLONDONDDNLNDNN
OONDNNNNOOOONLONDONNDNLONDONNNNOOLO
ONDNNLNLNODDNLNOOOLODNNODOLDNNDOOOO
OOONONDOLLONDONLDONNONLOLNNLLNOODNN
NLNODNDONNONDNNODLOLONDONNOOONONNON
NLONLONDONNNONNOOOOLLONONNLLLNNOONO
DDOOONOLONDONNNNLONDONNNOODNONNDODL
OLONLONDONOLLNNLLONDONNDNLONDONONLL
LONDONNDLNDDDNONOONOOLNDOOODDONONOD
ONLLONDONNNLONDONOONNOONLNLDOODONLL

Decrypted original text from the previous page:
JULIUS CAESAR

Mark and count: JULIA

```
QQXGWTJULIAKOQJULIACTDDRJSJULIANQTG
DJULIAFEUKNZKTZNBANZWZKHPHDMOJULIAF
KMBHVGVMJULIAWLYOCKKBJULIANIQBDUFDZ
MBYKRJXJAJULIAQABJULIAUZGJULIAJULIA
ZJULIAJULIASEOJWEFYXKOAJULIAOJUPNNW
LJULIAQTDJULIAJULIAVEVACQGUMKEHLAXL
TJULIAHYXUEZQMULVZPBMBLSIHGUGQSARPY
VRMXJULIAQJULIAZFOWLIFMGQRXLYZHFTKT
ZUHDFKABUQMZUXSPQPJULIAGGXTXSFATTGE
GJOOOFHXZLQVOMWLKMJULIAGVRKIBGIEVBK
RIILLVSKLRJUTLFJWMJLAWCFQJFORKGGSJT
DJULIAEJULIAGGJMQSDIYHMLRHLOQMEYAAZ
JULIALDYWORSVWABXMLJDTLKGTVEZAPYGXF
ZZBEKHFYCNHFJULIALISHGJULIAOWFAMRAU
TGZHMXVVJULIATFMHWWOEUYHHOFXALWCONR
CJULIAJRHQEPPJULIAOIDIOZEZLDSSVGCHE
OPXDUWSZBFCNNTDQEVIPZJQBAZHGJBCMYIW
VPTQRAJULIAWRJULIAPYEKJGIPMFHJDJOFV
AENQLFEDXNUNMJJULIAKGXKWSJEJULIAULS
OHIZWMTMAJULIASCGWJNKJPAHEDOOJFRFWO
FANSHZSEZMFGPYTOAXZLIDTXOYQWUNUQAGL
VGLAOREQJULIANLJWLRJULIAUUEYVFBDXRV
YIJULIALYGZEMCAPFRZVGJULIAHBUANBMYH
TBJULIAKFARTZSRAQHUVEDWBWGOUJULIAHI
NBLBNSIJULIAEKOAGTAWWUOBLLJULIAHOQI
IIOJULIAYYAMJYEEKYJIXNBHGAHMBUMWJFI
VCPWUUIMXRIOITIOPFIBECGYWVPYYJSCCTB
PJPBVGVETEGJULIALAYUJULIAJIHLDOMHHJ
ANUEBJECMRSXDRDDGQYFRRETBSGWHLQDQUX
```

24	14
11	9
26	24
42	18
40	15
80	32
0	35
12	5
63	12
12	16
54	12
56	10
4	4
1	13
20	20
36	0
40	7
0	23
45	18
21	25

Are you sure? See page 194!

CALCULATE

5 + 14 = _____	6 • 3 = _____
2 • 3 = _____	12 - 5 = _____
2 • 7 = _____	30 - 9 = _____
18 - 14 = _____	7 + 12 = _____
6 + 2 = _____	7 + 19 = _____
3 • 8 = _____	4 + 11 = _____
3 • 3 = _____	23 - 15 = _____
14 - 4 = _____	27 - 17 = _____
5 + 6 = _____	9 • 3 = _____
5 • 2 = _____	7 • 6 = _____
4 + 16 = _____	9 + 15 = _____
2 • 5 = _____	18 - 6 = _____
6 • 4 = _____	11 + 17 = _____
5 + 11 = _____	9 + 18 = _____
3 • 2 = _____	14 - 6 = _____
2 + 13 = _____	27 - 26 = _____
3 + 13 = _____	8 + 20 = _____
4 • 4 = _____	8 • 6 = _____
13 + 7 = _____	7 • 3 = _____
14 - 2 = _____	10 • 3 = _____

day 3

Additional tasks - only for math lovers!

50 - 26 = ____	5 + 9 = ____
20 - 9 = ____	4 + 5 = ____
6 + 20 = ____	3 • 8 = ____
6 • 7 = ____	5 + 13 = ____
31 + 9 = ____	5 • 3 = ____
10 • 8 = ____	4 • 8 = ____
17 - 17 = ____	5 • 7 = ____
6 + 6 = ____	29 - 24 = ____
9 • 7 = ____	16 - 4 = ____
2 • 6 = ____	2 • 8 = ____
17 + 37 = ____	6 • 2 = ____
7 • 8 = ____	5 • 2 = ____
2 • 2 = ____	17 - 13 = ____
31 - 30 = ____	22 - 9 = ____
11 + 9 = ____	2 • 10 = ____
41 - 5 = ____	6 - 6 = ____
4 • 10 = ____	11 - 4 = ____
42 - 42 = ____	7 + 16 = ____
5 • 9 = ____	25 - 7 = ____
7 + 14 = ____	20 + 5 = ____

FIND THE NUMBERS!

19	18
6	7
14	21
4	19
8	26
24	15
9	8
10	10
11	27
10	42
20	24
10	12
24	28
16	27
6	8
15	1
16	28
16	48
20	21
12	30

Mark and count: 7

```
9 5 9 1 9 3 6 5 6 0 5 4 4 1 0 9 0 7
8 7 1 1 4 8 0 8 9 4 7 8 7 6 8 1 2 5
6 1 7 4 4 0 6 9 0 9 5 6 9 0 6 0 0 0
8 7 5 5 3 5 2 8 8 0 6 6 1 2 6 8 8 8
2 9 6 6 9 1 1 9 5 1 9 0 0 1 2 2 6 8
2 9 9 8 6 3 0 1 5 0 4 3 4 2 4 2 0 3
6 5 6 5 7 3 7 6 6 3 9 9 6 5 5 2 4 4
8 7 9 2 7 2 1 6 0 2 7 0 4 2 6 6 8 6
5 8 8 3 6 4 8 8 1 4 7 2 9 2 8 6 6 4
1 0 7 4 6 0 3 1 1 5 2 0 6 0 2 2 7 5
2 4 9 5 4 9 4 6 8 2 6 6 6 5 3 3 5 6
2 7 9 7 0 0 9 8 3 0 2 6 5 3 9 2 4 9
3 2 8 3 8 3 0 4 4 0 2 8 9 1 7 0 8 9
```

Mark and count: 65

```
36 99 59 46 89 62 77 14 72 33 98 95
97 29 21 23 65 98 16 65 39 97 29 84
53 63 65 46 21 65 65 25 50 65 65 49
78 32 46 80 57 46 57 95 17 78 34 71
57 24 98 85 65 65 10 56 65 94 62 30
53 56 57 65 97 26 32 54 65 72 35 23
19 65 89 75 99 65 65 18 56 35 62 31
86 54 65 65 84 24 18 79 87 76 56 83
65 60 13 65 64 63 27 39 94 96 72 85
73 75 24 22 30 99 41 83 33 49 71 68
78 45 75 98 11 49 43 87 32 61 52 42
29 65 65 64 33 79 18 65 69 12 47 75
24 20 24 60 11 93 54 47 55 31 27 66
```

42 Are you sure? See page 195!

Now make a simple sketch of the memorized picture with as many details as possible:

TRY TO REMEMBER!

What should you find?

- City: _____
- Name: _____
- Decrypted text: _____

day 4

WARM UP!

$2 \cdot 3 =$ _____ $7 - 7 =$ _____

$9 + 10 =$ _____ $19 + 11 =$ _____

$7 + 7 =$ _____ $14 - 14 =$ _____

$18 - 5 =$ _____ $22 - 21 =$ _____

$10 + 9 =$ _____ $2 \cdot 4 =$ _____

$18 - 16 =$ _____ $3 \cdot 6 =$ _____

$9 + 3 =$ _____ $23 - 9 =$ _____

$4 - 4 =$ _____ $7 \cdot 4 =$ _____

$8 + 10 =$ _____ $8 \cdot 3 =$ _____

$11 - 2 =$ _____ $22 - 10 =$ _____

$3 \cdot 7 =$ _____ $9 \cdot 5 =$ _____

$2 + 17 =$ _____ $18 + 11 =$ _____

$6 + 9 =$ _____ $2 \cdot 6 =$ _____

$18 - 14 =$ _____ $29 - 9 =$ _____

$9 \cdot 2 =$ _____ $3 \cdot 9 =$ _____

$11 + 4 =$ _____ $25 - 11 =$ _____

$16 + 3 =$ _____ $21 - 13 =$ _____

$8 + 8 =$ _____ $15 - 5 =$ _____

$19 - 2 =$ _____ $13 + 12 =$ _____

$10 - 5 =$ _____ $3 \cdot 10 =$ _____

Decipher the following code with the "Caesar encryption".

The required character offset to the right is: 1

T R D C Z S G H R

_ _ _ _ _ _ _ _ _

Copy the decrypted text on page 197.

ABCDEFGHIJKLMNOPQRSTUVWXYZ_ABCDEF

Memorize this picture and all of its details as best as you can to make a sketch of it later.

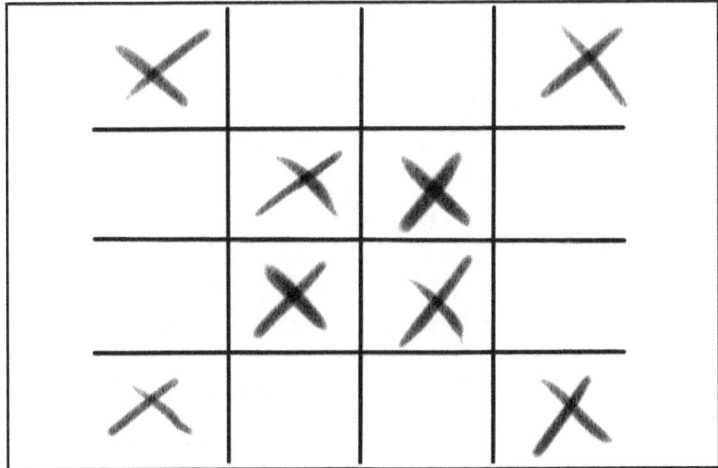

6	0
19	30
14	0
13	1
19	8
2	18
12	14
0	28
18	24
9	12
21	45
19	29
15	12
4	20
18	27
15	14
19	8
16	10
17	25
5	30

Mark and count: E

```
BBBBBBBBBBBEBEBBBBBEBBBBBEBEEBBBEB
BBBBBBBBBBBBBBBBEBBBBBBBBBBEBBBBBBB
BBEBBBBEBEBBBBBBBBBEBBBBEBBBBBBBBBB
BBBBBBBBBBEBBBBBBEBBBBBBBBBBBBEBBBB
BBBBBBBBBBBBBBBBBEBBBBBBBBBBBBBBBBB
BBBBBBBBBBBBBEBBBBBBBEEBBBBBBBBBBBB
BBBBBBBBBBBBBBBBBBBBBBBBBBBBBBBBBBB
BBBEBBBBBBBBBBBBBBEBBBBBBBBBBBBBBBB
BBBBEBBBBBBBBBBBBBBBBBBBBBBBBBBBBBB
BBBBBEBBBBBBBBEBBBBBBBBBBBBBBBBEBB
BEBBBBBBBBEBBBBBEBBBBBBBBBBBBBBBE
BBBBBBBBBBBBBBBBBBBBBBBBBBBBBBBBBBB
BBBBEBBBEBBBBBBBBBBBBBBBBBBBBBBBBB
```

Mark and count: SYDNEY

```
SYSYYYNYNSEDSNEESSSYYSYYEEEDYYEESEY
DEDDDNSNSYDNEYSYDYYSEEYENNSYDNEYYYE
DSNSDNYYEEYSYDNEYNEDDYEYYNDNDDEEDYY
NDSYYYYSNEDDSYDNEYYSNENEDEEYSYSYYYE
DYENSYDNEYEDYYNYNYYSYDNEYYSYSEEYDES
YYDEYYEYSYDNEYEYSYDNEYNENYEDNNYDYYY
ESYDNEYYYSEEYYEEEESYDNEYSSYDNEYEEEE
EYYNEDSYDNEYNSYNYSYYNSSYDNEYYYENDEY
YEYDSSYSYDNEYDEDSSYSYDNEYNSYDYSESYS
ESNNESNNYSNYYNEDNSDSYDNEYYNSNSYDNEY
ESYDNEYYEESNDYSYDNEYEDYSYDNEYDDYYYN
DYYNEENNSENSYDNEYSYDNEYESNDDNNSSDSS
YYNYYSYEYYSYDNEYYDYSSESNNNYDYEDNDDS
```

48

Decrypted original text from the previous page:
USED THIS

Mark and count: LEWIS

```
YZLNELXMWPAUAALEWISITEQHKRJLEWISMZB
EFELBBVZMTWYOEGJRJVEDOBGUJZJLEWISJW
AVOSBGDTLWTNAZGCQMQGEGHLEWISXLEWISY
UNVDMZJVACUIUKASKYQCNKWCGCMRNCYEOMK
YAXIXLFGLEWISTBJHRVFHELEWISJLOPGVIN
PQHPXDIISKYFBGZLEWISLEWISZBLMBRUDMW
WLEWISLXYMCPFMHTMYCUEKXKEKOTXKSSDFT
UMRTVXWGBISDCHNLBVTMKEUORFTSLEWISMZ
BSHQFLEWISLEWISOWLEWISJTQFIEALLEWIS
RYIELEWISBDSBOTHHENDIRKQFZUYNXKXWPH
GNBLEWISZUTNAURGRERVVRPKCRMGLEWISBC
UAJZVULEWISAMKEJGIGOXBLEWISTVIDNOKW
VHGXHJYKPLEWISCDNGTNKHLQUMLEWISHQNQ
KXHSJTFLKGTYNWWMGWTTTPEVVKNFHDLEWIS
JDQEKMIMXYPGXOMCSXIIAOWCUZFJJLEWISQ
EHHXHDEEKNTCOMGSWFJMJLNPYLEWISSCFZY
SLEWISZIZLEWISTRORVVJTCNMUGUSYUWIKP
DKAAKNTJPIYPNKFBLXKLEWISVFHLEWISJGT
IWFIRLQFJRRKEBDBJFKLEWISQLIBAZLEWIS
JFUDVOSAGBVXLEWISYLMMJSDIPLEWISHEGO
XRALNIZFMFJACLEWISFBLEWISKMRCGJFUZB
SIYEJNGOAYPIEIXMZZAKOGAZLEWISPERRQK
JMOOFHLEWISDIFWHLOHMJXEICEBTDNASFHJ
PPRMQBXLEWISWRULEWISVGFKGLEWISQIDHB
FLEWISMXCNEPQRNBWGQYURQXQYAPVMVDDHV
FFLEWISMPGLEWISXNSNZLEWISTGLSPUXFSF
KKKRCLYWWTIHOCKLHDCXRLADWSQTADTVTAI
KDZKMLSAMOSCSTZDSWILEWISTQNVWKJUSAK
MNNHBVIVYKAFZPBZZDZZMDSCLEWISVXXXPG
```

46	40
38	13
49	18
30	21
12	9
4	18
21	5
13	11
33	16
10	49
19	30
40	21
24	28
56	20
4	14
90	21
42	21
9	0
16	0
51	25

Are you sure? See page 194!

CALCULATE

3 + 14 = _____	8 + 15 = _____
10 + 6 = _____	6 + 7 = _____
6 + 14 = _____	28 - 21 = _____
3 + 16 = _____	9 + 18 = _____
13 - 6 = _____	30 - 29 = _____
3 • 4 = _____	9 - 8 = _____
2 • 3 = _____	2 • 7 = _____
6 • 3 = _____	18 + 6 = _____
4 • 5 = _____	5 • 3 = _____
18 - 18 = _____	8 + 9 = _____
2 • 4 = _____	4 + 4 = _____
18 - 12 = _____	12 + 17 = _____
5 + 15 = _____	5 • 7 = _____
11 - 8 = _____	20 - 8 = _____
4 + 15 = _____	3 • 5 = _____
9 • 2 = _____	9 + 12 = _____
4 • 2 = _____	20 - 9 = _____
4 + 8 = _____	19 + 7 = _____
6 - 5 = _____	24 - 16 = _____
4 + 5 = _____	11 - 10 = _____

Additional tasks - only for math lovers!

$17 + 29 =$ _____ $4 \cdot 10 =$ _____

$29 + 9 =$ _____ $21 - 8 =$ _____

$34 + 15 =$ _____ $9 \cdot 2 =$ _____

$10 \cdot 3 =$ _____ $6 + 15 =$ _____

$32 - 20 =$ _____ $17 - 8 =$ _____

$12 - 8 =$ _____ $3 \cdot 6 =$ _____

$34 - 13 =$ _____ $28 - 23 =$ _____

$49 - 36 =$ _____ $22 - 11 =$ _____

$18 + 15 =$ _____ $4 \cdot 4 =$ _____

$2 \cdot 5 =$ _____ $7 \cdot 7 =$ _____

$9 + 10 =$ _____ $5 \cdot 6 =$ _____

$8 \cdot 5 =$ _____ $17 + 4 =$ _____

$8 \cdot 3 =$ _____ $8 + 20 =$ _____

$38 + 18 =$ _____ $2 \cdot 10 =$ _____

$2 \cdot 2 =$ _____ $5 + 9 =$ _____

$10 \cdot 9 =$ _____ $7 + 14 =$ _____

$7 \cdot 6 =$ _____ $3 \cdot 7 =$ _____

$28 - 19 =$ _____ $7 - 7 =$ _____

$8 \cdot 2 =$ _____ $22 - 22 =$ _____

$30 + 21 =$ _____ $12 + 13 =$ _____

FIND THE NUMBERS!

17	23
16	13
20	7
19	27
7	1
12	1
6	14
18	24
20	15
0	17
8	8
6	29
20	35
3	12
19	15
18	21
8	11
12	26
1	8
9	1

Mark and count: 3

```
0 6 2 1 3 6 7 5 8 3 1 8 3 5 9 1 0 4
8 4 8 2 7 1 8 5 5 3 7 2 5 6 8 5 1 4
8 9 2 9 5 2 5 5 9 1 2 1 7 4 0 2 1 6
4 5 4 2 0 3 1 9 0 6 0 5 4 8 3 5 0 5
0 5 9 5 1 1 9 0 3 8 2 3 9 3 9 4 2 6
3 2 3 4 1 7 5 5 2 7 4 9 8 6 7 1 4 1
1 0 5 6 9 9 5 4 7 3 2 4 3 6 6 6 4 6
4 3 9 6 5 3 3 3 7 7 0 8 8 0 1 8 2 4
3 6 1 7 7 4 1 8 1 6 7 1 5 5 8 0 0 7
2 2 3 0 5 4 7 0 9 8 4 9 0 8 2 0 2 5
7 8 5 2 8 0 9 6 2 0 8 0 8 3 3 5 0 3
5 7 7 2 1 7 4 3 3 8 9 5 6 1 1 5 2 6
3 8 9 2 8 9 4 8 4 5 1 4 6 4 5 8 3 5
```

Mark and count: 77

```
40 56 67 54 16 24 38 40 93 32 93 60
42 27 87 40 50 74 75 61 49 74 56 70
20 77 13 32 70 48 56 90 65 57 88 32
76 77 39 32 77 77 92 23 81 27 58 48
86 19 63 46 75 54 12 88 63 15 64 12
70 96 41 56 99 37 77 68 24 26 49 12
56 72 30 94 46 80 45 18 55 29 83 80
25 61 88 77 85 35 14 21 27 96 86 50
67 20 52 74 18 88 39 28 30 17 31 35
64 77 50 87 18 96 13 49 25 73 39 16
65 39 38 37 77 81 21 49 12 70 99 40
77 46 44 77 58 72 68 24 77 61 83 79
12 77 72 39 45 77 93 87 69 24 77 77
```

Are you sure? See page 195!

Now make a simple sketch of the memorized picture with as many details as possible:

TRY TO REMEMBER!

What should you find?

- City: _____
- Name: _____
- Decrypted text: _____

day 5

WARM UP!

2 • 9 = _____	7 • 4 = _____
7 + 11 = _____	8 + 21 = _____
2 - 2 = _____	9 • 5 = _____
7 + 10 = _____	2 • 7 = _____
3 • 4 = _____	6 • 4 = _____
2 + 7 = _____	29 - 4 = _____
17 - 16 = _____	9 + 19 = _____
14 - 12 = _____	11 + 14 = _____
20 - 19 = _____	16 - 12 = _____
6 • 2 = _____	9 + 8 = _____
2 + 4 = _____	6 • 3 = _____
8 + 7 = _____	20 - 3 = _____
2 • 3 = _____	24 + 4 = _____
10 - 9 = _____	28 - 12 = _____
20 - 7 = _____	5 + 5 = _____
10 • 2 = _____	3 • 3 = _____
15 - 4 = _____	11 + 7 = _____
4 • 3 = _____	17 - 4 = _____
4 • 5 = _____	16 + 6 = _____
18 - 17 = _____	4 • 8 = _____

Decipher the following code with the "Caesar encryption".

The required character offset to the right is: 6

M S M N Z G U _ I L

_ _ _ _ _ _ _ _ _ _

Copy the decrypted text on page 197.

ABCDEFGHIJKLMNOPQRSTUVWXYZ_ABCDEF

Memorize this picture and all of its details as best as you can to make a sketch of it later.

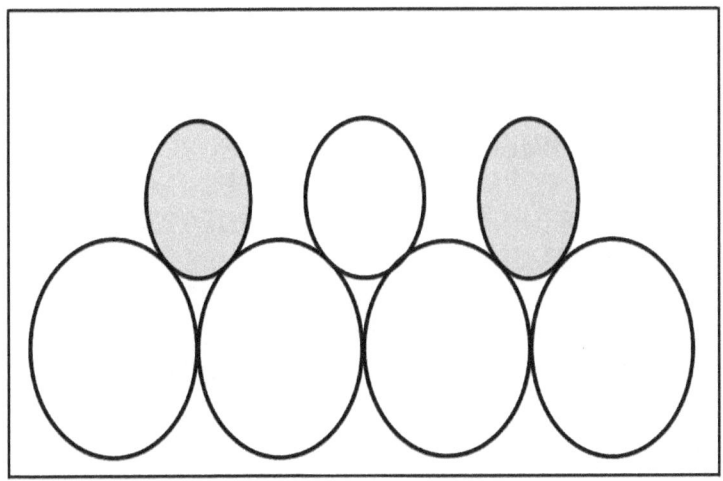

18	28
18	29
0	45
17	14
12	24
9	25
1	28
2	25
1	4
12	17
6	18
15	17
6	28
1	16
13	10
20	9
11	18
12	13
20	22
1	32

Mark and count: G

```
OOOOOOOOOOOOOOOOOOOOOOOOOOGOOOOOGOOO
OGOOOGOOOOOOOOOOOOOOOOOOOOOOOOOGOOO
OGOOOOOOOOOOOOOOOOOOOOOOOGOOOOOOOOOO
OOOOOOOOOOOOOOOOOOOOOOOOOOOOOOOOOOOO
OOOOOOOOOOOOOOOOOOOOOOOOOOOOOOOOOOOO
OOOOOOOOOOOOOOOGOGOOOOOOOGOOOOOOOOO
OOOOOOOOOOOOOOOOOOOOOOOGOGOOOOOOOOO
GOOOOOOOOOOOOOOOOOOOOOOOOOGOOOOOOOO
OGOOOOOOOOOOOOGOOOOOOOOOOOOOOOOGOOO
OGOOOOOOOOOOOOOOOOOOOOOOOOOOOOOOOOO
OOOOOOOOOOOOOOOOOOOGOOOOOOOOOOOO
OOOOOOOOOOOOOOOOOOOOOOOOOOOOOOOOOOOO
OOOOOOOOOOOGOOOOOOOOOOOGOOOOOOOOOO
```

Mark and count: ROME

```
EMREMEEOEROOMRMMMOOEOOEOEROMEMMOMRO
ROOOMOREMEROMEMOROMRMORROMEROMEOORE
EMEMOROMEERREMOEMERREORRRMMRREMEORO
REEEOOMMORMOEROMEMEMMEMORMMEMRROMEE
ROMEOEOOOMEERROEERREROMEOEOROMEERMEE
OROEOMEREORMROMEMEEMROMEEMMROMEEEOM
EMREMEOMROMROMEMROOROMEOOERRROEROME
ERMRMOOROROMEORREMMRRRMROOEMERRRO
MOOOROREEOMMEEEMEOEMROMERREOERRMMOR
ORROMEROMEOOMMMREEOOROMEEOERMMERRMO
MOOROOOMORMOOMEMEMORMOMOROOEMMEOEMR
EMRREORMRROORRMRMOROMERMROMEOEOOEE
RREOOROMROMRORORRROMEOMMORRORMRMOER
```

Decrypted original text from the previous page:
SYSTEM FOR

Mark and count: ALEX

```
IIBLMXPSRYGHYBALEXALEXAEHQVQFAIVKDO
EIALEXCIMALEXHGJMIOALEXDLHPNTUKOJJV
JPPVALEXFNKCCYBQOVTICEIZAPPANAPLBVL
RREXNCOVDYGIQJKERCZBKGGTJKLFCJOALEX
QMHHTKALEXOAPZOYPVGEOXIDALEXLMTJMUB
CZMWOSPMUBQKKMERNMTIALEXJVMURFVWJGU
RXALEXNKVPNYUNTVALEXHZYSWLPDBGEPWZD
APXWCSXKTHOTTQNSJFDLMDNPALEXSSWNERG
ZFLFHUIAVUZUZYSBCYPCBFGZZENALEXRHVN
XVQLXEULNFHNQMQAVRALEXIIDFHMPPHPRIM
ABDXHLGZFPQAOALEXYSFALEXSSALEXIWOMF
ERJAMVVKXITQLXEDJQKZYYUGPFPHZFBUXVB
YVJJQPOYHFXOPODGSKTWNNAEIOTUUKALEXS
LKALEXNVZFQWTALEXTHYYGTIGWTSBZPCGJP
QAHRCKAFPVJFXKSAPNPHODCUJFPMLPQPUMZ
ODDUOCRFFYEVIUZKBNIBJENHOTALEXKRBJH
AWJRJMNQGDBCIUHGXZALEXLLOJALEXBFUFW
ALEXINZLGKXIGOBRPFTVKTVALEXOQGLKCOP
JPLNSLCCQOTAXTASJEXALEXZAMWTYKZUYAI
BCWSJMIMACKYTSUALEXHVRTSZNUFGZWQOFL
OGRHLRDFSIXALEXJFCECPZNVFMSPHNIPQUH
GASGAVFKWMALEXHPALEXFFLLQPZSXLGMLZW
GTMVKQOLFXDALEXALEXUOJVCQQKGVLSJMLB
JEHSRPCAOPIOGQRLQENPHXPUADBFQJBMLVQ
ALEXHNALEXLVPPUBDUMPDJJSTALEXTBTINR
ALEXVTAFSUZIBDMPAJVQPGZUIWCGTTNVDDW
YVOBMORQNREHALEXALEXOSTBJUCUGKMPHKA
SELSCTALEXFRFRKVZKMFALEXUTMHSSZDKCU
SWFAEPRAPNQUALPZRFUGVPDYIPVCNAUVZMK
```

18	3
21	12
21	32
54	36
48	24
35	21
5	25
37	24
20	1
45	2
4	29
30	27
5	0
27	25
43	14
63	29
19	22
48	20
31	7
15	19

Are you sure? See page 194!

CALCULATE

12 − 10 = _____	6 + 11 = _____
3 • 2 = _____	20 + 8 = _____
6 • 3 = _____	19 + 7 = _____
9 • 2 = _____	3 • 5 = _____
4 • 4 = _____	19 − 10 = _____
17 − 12 = _____	20 + 10 = _____
4 • 5 = _____	9 • 5 = _____
2 + 6 = _____	3 • 9 = _____
3 • 3 = _____	5 + 22 = _____
2 • 3 = _____	24 − 7 = _____
2 • 6 = _____	4 + 9 = _____
8 • 2 = _____	2 • 9 = _____
4 • 2 = _____	24 − 18 = _____
15 − 3 = _____	5 + 18 = _____
12 − 2 = _____	27 − 16 = _____
5 + 10 = _____	6 • 2 = _____
15 − 7 = _____	12 + 17 = _____
4 • 6 = _____	6 • 6 = _____
5 + 7 = _____	20 − 17 = _____
5 • 2 = _____	16 + 8 = _____

Additional tasks - only for math lovers!

$23 - 5 =$ _____	$8 - 5 =$ _____
$7 \cdot 3 =$ _____	$30 - 18 =$ _____
$7 + 14 =$ _____	$8 \cdot 4 =$ _____
$9 \cdot 6 =$ _____	$4 \cdot 9 =$ _____
$14 + 34 =$ _____	$19 + 5 =$ _____
$11 + 24 =$ _____	$29 - 8 =$ _____
$16 - 11 =$ _____	$5 \cdot 5 =$ _____
$24 + 13 =$ _____	$29 - 5 =$ _____
$10 \cdot 2 =$ _____	$13 - 12 =$ _____
$25 + 20 =$ _____	$7 - 5 =$ _____
$37 - 33 =$ _____	$18 + 11 =$ _____
$15 + 15 =$ _____	$30 - 3 =$ _____
$12 - 7 =$ _____	$29 - 29 =$ _____
$44 - 17 =$ _____	$17 + 8 =$ _____
$19 + 24 =$ _____	$2 \cdot 7 =$ _____
$7 \cdot 9 =$ _____	$15 + 14 =$ _____
$44 - 25 =$ _____	$25 - 3 =$ _____
$28 + 20 =$ _____	$4 \cdot 5 =$ _____
$13 + 18 =$ _____	$26 - 19 =$ _____
$47 - 32 =$ _____	$14 + 5 =$ _____

FIND THE NUMBERS!

2	17
6	28
18	26
18	15
16	9
5	30
20	45
8	27
9	27
6	17
12	13
16	18
8	6
12	23
10	11
15	12
8	29
24	36
12	3
10	24

Mark and count: 4

```
8 0 4 0 7 3 1 0 0 9 0 0 6 9 3 2 9 5
0 2 3 0 9 9 1 1 1 0 2 5 2 6 8 2 5 7
6 3 9 0 9 8 6 6 4 4 5 1 1 2 8 4 0 2
5 7 1 6 7 6 8 4 7 2 5 2 4 0 8 2 7 1
5 2 7 6 6 4 7 2 8 7 9 0 2 4 8 0 2 1
7 7 5 5 0 4 8 7 5 5 5 3 4 3 7 4 0 7
0 4 6 7 1 8 7 5 2 8 5 7 9 0 3 2 3 0
6 9 1 6 2 6 1 8 6 4 5 7 7 1 0 9 2 3
7 0 1 3 9 1 0 3 5 2 7 0 5 0 8 8 9 0
4 4 8 5 9 4 5 7 2 7 0 3 9 9 9 6 1 7
7 6 0 4 5 9 4 7 9 9 2 2 3 9 7 0 8 2
5 9 9 9 4 3 0 6 6 2 1 0 9 5 0 3 3 7
2 1 7 3 7 1 8 1 6 5 9 9 7 6 5 2 5 0
```

Mark and count: 12

```
32 48 18 94 32 28 47 86 96 21 12 12
36 45 23 26 72 80 86 85 12 81 41 81
24 50 49 24 14 83 12 51 36 97 72 82
19 12 58 44 69 57 12 52 63 56 90 93
63 95 12 11 89 70 91 12 58 42 89 99
43 81 56 87 76 18 23 96 87 82 49 15
49 46 35 61 50 35 54 70 12 27 69 68
70 12 54 87 18 71 69 86 85 88 89 98
12 61 81 41 21 12 25 77 66 59 41 75
22 96 11 17 65 99 74 12 76 29 35 38
47 90 49 90 78 90 50 92 81 95 71 17
62 58 72 29 10 12 57 63 63 31 31 50
59 20 42 80 12 25 45 29 17 12 12 30
```

Are you sure? See page 195!

Now make a simple sketch of the memorized picture
with as many details as possible:

```




```

TRY TO REMEMBER!

What should you find?

- City: _____
- Name: _____
- Decrypted text: _____

day 6

WARM UP!

5 • 2 = ____	24 - 4 = ____
20 - 8 = ____	18 - 5 = ____
11 + 4 = ____	27 - 24 = ____
12 - 2 = ____	7 • 7 = ____
4 + 10 = ____	15 + 7 = ____
2 + 7 = ____	29 - 20 = ____
2 • 2 = ____	23 + 7 = ____
18 - 3 = ____	5 • 9 = ____
13 - 9 = ____	18 - 6 = ____
16 - 9 = ____	25 - 7 = ____
7 • 2 = ____	30 - 25 = ____
2 • 3 = ____	5 • 4 = ____
3 • 4 = ____	8 • 6 = ____
5 + 8 = ____	12 + 9 = ____
6 - 3 = ____	21 - 21 = ____
8 • 2 = ____	17 - 4 = ____
16 + 2 = ____	3 • 6 = ____
9 - 7 = ____	9 - 3 = ____
2 • 4 = ____	6 • 3 = ____
4 • 3 = ____	7 + 13 = ____

Decipher the following code with the "Caesar encryption".

The required character offset to the right is: 4

I E H E P X N U

_ _ _ _ _ _ _ _

Copy the decrypted text on page 197.

ABCDEFGHIJKLMNOPQRSTUVWXYZ_ABCDEF

Memorize this picture and all of its details as best as you can to make a sketch of it later.

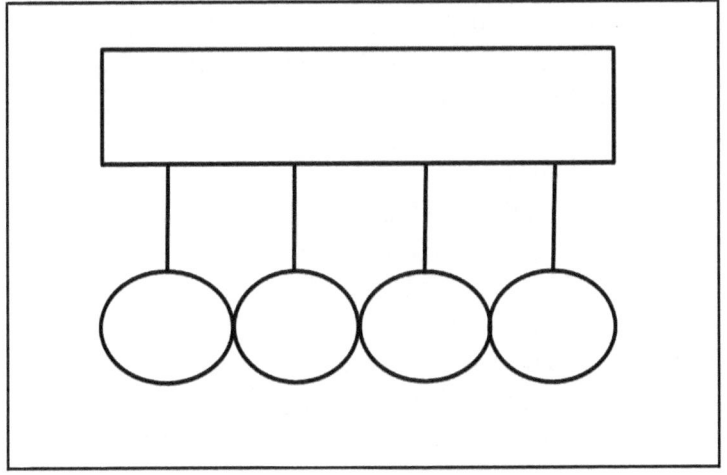

10	20
12	13
15	3
10	49
14	22
9	9
4	30
15	45
4	12
7	18
14	5
6	20
12	48
13	21
3	0
16	13
18	18
2	6
8	18
12	20

Mark and count: T

```
TIIIIIIIIIIIIIIIIIIIIIIIIIIIIIIIIITI
IIIITIIIIIIIIIIIIIIIIIIIIIIIIIIIIIII
IIIIIIIIITIIIIIIIIIIITIIIIIIIIIIIIII
IIIIITIIIIIIIIIIIIIIIIITIIIIIIIIIIII
IIITIIIIIIIIIIIIITITIIIIIIIIIIIIIIII
IIIIIIIIIIIIIIIIIIIIIITIIIITIIIIIIII
IIIIIIIIIIIIIIIIIIIIIIIIIIIIIIIIIIII
IIIIIIIIIIITIIIIIIIIIIIIIIIIIIIIIIII
IIIIIIITIIIIIIIIIIIIIIIIIIIIIIIIIIII
IIIIIIIIIIIIIIIIIIIIIIIIIIITIIIIIIII
IITIIIIIIIIIIIIIIIIIIIIIIIIIIIIIIIII
IITIIIIIIITIIIIIIIIIIIIIIIIIIIIIIIII
```

Mark and count: BEIJING

```
GBENIBBEEJEIIBEBBEEINEGIEIEIJBIIIEJ
NNBIBGBEIJINGIEINEBEIJINGGNJIEIIJBG
NNENJIJEBBGGIEBENBEIJINGBBBEIJINGGN
GBGJNBIEGIBJJGENIBIBEIJINGJNENEEIIB
JNBEIJINGGIINIJNNNBNJNIEIENNNJIIBBI
IBEIJINGBEIJINGJBEIGBGIGGJIBJEJJEIJ
IIBEIJINGIBEIJINGIGBBEIJINGJBGNEBNI
IBEIJINGEJJIIIBGIGIEGJBIEIGNNINEBIN
BGJGJIEIENIBIIBIIIENGIEIBEIJINGGBEI
NBNEBJJEBNBEGEIJIEIEEBGIEIGJEJBJEIE
IBGGBEIJINGNNEBNIIBENBEIJINGBIIIGIG
NGBIIJJBBEIIIBENJBGJJIBBJJJNNINNBIB
EBBEIJINGIBNGIJJJGENBEIJINGEIBNBBNJ
```

Decrypted original text from the previous page:
MILITARY

Mark and count: SYBILLE

```
CTDGMTTPOEMVOSGTEZNJFJNCTLEWSFOPDJU
HOGGUCIADDKRZNTPSYBILLEPWFDESYBILLE
IISYBILLEKHHNGTEVDOWSYBILLESYBILLEL
ODTCZXYJAGSYBILLETNRKZFYNRURYJBAWBC
LRIHJGBTKJSQUOLSERNHSYBILLECZTYEDPE
SEHTUWDIDVZZCHQXZPZISNPAJZOHIJRGCQN
EMHEQMYJAGNFOQINGHGUFTFVMSYBILLEWJX
GQRPISIIHBQWHBNNHVLSYBILLEQPOWGGFYU
RCFZRPSYBILLELGAVEYPJFXDYZZNGRWFDKB
IPTJGTJDKBISYBILLEFDTXAIYSNHZCWBZTZ
OIWFMTBGZHJSBNNMOFSYBILLEHHIWZFRVEV
UISYBILLESPCZENDFNPDISSIBSYBILLEDRY
TIJDNDDSYBILLEJHVOSYBILLELCHPUVFOYQ
YCKQGCHIGPENPCQTYIUBIRQNJMPIOHRGLSP
TBMODWSZJZSDBVRVFZWCUUUTTNNUPKETYBE
ZMFWBYEFZXYFIJSYBILLEHMLOUSWZDEDRTJ
GHIFXBFZBZKAIZLSYBILLEMSLKFKXWFMIGR
ZCPJIJZBEASYBILLEODLEZTSMYJBANIGJYQ
NXQQHEORAWHOHTTOJWWSYBILLEXSNMJSEIA
TILCEBNGBQDVFPTWIRYOTUXCXEURNEYVCZB
SQSIKBPVQNSILHQHIXUSYBILLESYBILLELF
BLOJZXDGMBSYBILLETISYBILLERNCXVXIYG
DAASDLXSYBILLEOUYEERSYBILLEJSYBILLE
LDKXSYBILLEEIFCRRUFAVTQMCXNNEHXHWVL
OLLAJFAKOKVQPEUOTHADTZLESYBILLEXIMZ
XFUVMCSLUNEGSYBILLELSYBILLEQMCZWTXC
KRPDVCHVVNZLJCJDIQBFSYBILLEBLVWFKHQ
QISIXIPTFTRDSYBILLETSYBILLEBZKCTNCL
LRJTHFMYYUHIRSYBILLESYBILLEINQGGDUE
```

27	7
50	20
36	2
4	9
53	7
53	29
52	17
30	6
10	24
11	22
60	12
54	14
57	8
37	21
42	24
2	8
28	12
49	29
10	32
72	10

Are you sure? See page 194!

CALCULATE

18 - 6 = _____	12 + 10 = _____
6 + 8 = _____	14 + 10 = _____
2 + 17 = _____	9 + 10 = _____
4 + 16 = _____	8 • 6 = _____
16 - 3 = _____	18 + 9 = _____
15 + 2 = _____	19 + 11 = _____
6 • 3 = _____	9 + 13 = _____
15 - 6 = _____	15 + 10 = _____
14 - 7 = _____	8 • 5 = _____
7 • 2 = _____	4 + 11 = _____
10 + 5 = _____	6 + 10 = _____
8 • 3 = _____	8 + 6 = _____
19 - 3 = _____	7 • 7 = _____
14 - 9 = _____	27 - 9 = _____
18 - 13 = _____	3 • 3 = _____
2 + 10 = _____	3 • 2 = _____
13 + 6 = _____	19 + 4 = _____
3 + 11 = _____	29 - 22 = _____
19 - 6 = _____	8 + 13 = _____
3 • 4 = _____	30 - 21 = _____

Additional tasks - only for math lovers!

$9 \cdot 3 =$ _____ $21 - 14 =$ _____

$5 \cdot 10 =$ _____ $10 + 10 =$ _____

$9 \cdot 4 =$ _____ $19 - 17 =$ _____

$23 - 19 =$ _____ $19 - 10 =$ _____

$17 + 36 =$ _____ $20 - 13 =$ _____

$33 + 20 =$ _____ $8 + 21 =$ _____

$19 + 33 =$ _____ $20 - 3 =$ _____

$7 + 23 =$ _____ $2 \cdot 3 =$ _____

$28 - 18 =$ _____ $17 + 7 =$ _____

$32 - 21 =$ _____ $15 + 7 =$ _____

$36 + 24 =$ _____ $6 \cdot 2 =$ _____

$30 + 24 =$ _____ $25 - 11 =$ _____

$24 + 33 =$ _____ $2 \cdot 4 =$ _____

$11 + 26 =$ _____ $26 - 5 =$ _____

$35 + 7 =$ _____ $3 \cdot 8 =$ _____

$24 - 22 =$ _____ $4 \cdot 2 =$ _____

$4 \cdot 7 =$ _____ $2 \cdot 6 =$ _____

$13 + 36 =$ _____ $14 + 15 =$ _____

$2 \cdot 5 =$ _____ $8 \cdot 4 =$ _____

$8 \cdot 9 =$ _____ $15 - 5 =$ _____

12	22
14	24
19	19
20	48
13	27
17	30
18	22
9	25
7	40
14	15
15	16
24	14
16	49
5	18
5	9
12	6
19	23
14	7
13	21
12	9

Mark and count: 1

```
2 9 7 4 1 5 9 7 6 7 3 6 0 0 7 7 2 3
7 2 6 6 2 5 2 7 8 0 2 3 5 7 2 3 0 0
0 5 7 6 9 7 7 6 3 5 2 6 0 4 0 5 9 9
4 4 4 8 5 3 0 9 1 2 6 8 4 9 4 7 9 6
2 7 7 7 1 5 7 1 3 2 1 9 9 0 1 7 7 7
3 4 2 1 2 3 3 8 8 8 0 0 0 2 3 5 1 2
2 9 2 2 5 6 5 0 2 5 9 4 2 8 7 4 4 5
2 0 3 3 8 5 9 5 9 5 5 0 5 8 3 5 1 5
6 8 0 5 2 8 8 4 3 8 8 8 5 9 3 8 2 0
2 7 8 8 8 5 2 7 5 5 0 4 7 4 2 0 9 5
8 9 8 7 2 0 6 5 0 2 7 6 8 9 6 8 3 0
1 9 6 4 6 2 7 1 9 4 6 3 4 0 3 1 0 0
3 6 0 1 5 8 0 9 5 1 9 8 4 1 7 0 1 6
```

Mark and count: 33

```
96 89 90 94 61 24 52 24 38 43 94 12
87 33 33 56 55 82 28 72 33 62 33 28
49 44 13 11 91 84 34 62 10 46 13 90
73 47 73 56 76 37 49 54 65 33 13 89
41 33 28 54 90 19 96 89 33 52 98 34
70 66 70 40 32 96 55 75 13 12 17 92
89 81 99 33 53 69 50 42 54 49 37 94
32 65 32 90 71 51 70 33 70 86 28 96
46 35 26 15 67 33 82 33 76 72 56 60
13 72 88 57 57 15 43 75 30 74 90 80
33 76 96 67 24 10 44 39 67 94 55 69
71 36 25 41 79 23 78 80 33 10 38 14
73 99 65 55 17 50 90 33 84 88 30 80
```

 Are you sure? See page 195!

Now make a simple sketch of the memorized picture with as many details as possible:

TRY TO REMEMBER!

What should you find?

- City: _____
- Name: _____
- Decrypted text: _____

day 7

WARM UP!

6 + 9 = _____	4 • 6 = _____
5 - 2 = _____	7 - 6 = _____
13 + 4 = _____	4 • 7 = _____
2 • 9 = _____	5 • 8 = _____
20 - 19 = _____	12 - 9 = _____
19 - 9 = _____	2 • 10 = _____
11 - 11 = _____	7 • 4 = _____
13 - 3 = _____	10 - 4 = _____
3 - 2 = _____	7 + 19 = _____
3 + 16 = _____	12 + 11 = _____
5 + 4 = _____	12 - 10 = _____
2 • 2 = _____	21 - 5 = _____
13 - 7 = _____	4 + 24 = _____
3 • 2 = _____	8 + 15 = _____
9 + 5 = _____	14 + 13 = _____
20 - 4 = _____	12 + 6 = _____
17 - 8 = _____	23 + 6 = _____
19 - 16 = _____	23 - 18 = _____
5 + 9 = _____	16 + 7 = _____
8 • 2 = _____	14 - 10 = _____

Decipher the following code with the "Caesar encryption".

The required character offset to the right is: 4

Z K I I Q J E Z X P E K J

_ _ _ _ _ _ _ _ _ _ _ _ _

Copy the decrypted text on page 197.

ABCDEFGHIJKLMNOPQRSTUVWXYZ_ABCDEF

Memorize this picture and all of its details as best as you can to make a sketch of it later.

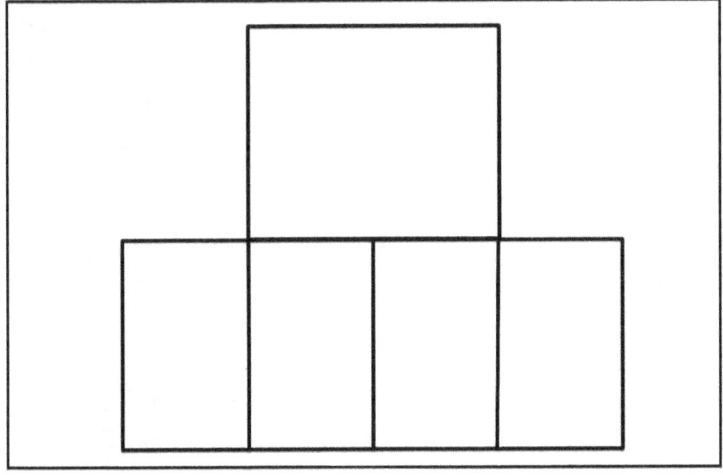

15 24

3 1

17 28

18 40

1 3

10 20

0 28

10 6

1 26

19 23

9 2

4 16

6 28

6 23

14 27

16 18

9 29

3 5

14 23

16 4

Mark and count: N

```
MMMMMMNMMMNMMMMMMMMMMMMMMMMMMMMMM
NMMMMMMMMMMMMMMMMMMMMMMMMMMMMMMMM
MMMMMMMMMMMNMMMMMMMMMMMMMMMMMMMMM
MMMMMMMMMMMMMMMMMMMMMMMMMNMMMMNMMM
MMMMMMMNMMMMMMMNMMMMMMMMMMMMMMMNM
MMMMMMMMMMMMMMMMMMMMMMMMMMMMMMMMM
MMMMMMMMMMMMMMMMMMMMMMMMMMMMMMMMM
MNMMMMMMMMMMMMMMMMMNMMMMMMMMMMN
MMMMMMMMMMMMMMMMMMMMMMMMMMMMMMM
MMMMMMMMMNMMMMMMMMMMMMMMMMMMMMM
MMMMMMNMMMMMMMMMMMMMMMMMMMMMMMM
MMMMMMMNMMMMMMMMMMMMNMMMMMMMMMM
MNMMMNMMMMMMMMMMMMMMMMMMMMMMMMM
```

Mark and count: VICTORIA

```
IVICTORIAITRARRIVICTORIAIOATCTATAOR
IVVICTORIAITIVICTORIAIIRAIITIOIIAAV
IOTVICTORIATTAIAOAROAVAAOOAVICTORIA
VVCVIITITRRVTRTITCVRAIRIOACVITICIAI
COVVTAIIIAOOIORVITCVITAICTAVTIIVOIV
VOVTTOOCIRIVITVOCTRRAOOCAITIOTIIAAO
ICVICTORIAOCIOAICOTATTCVVIVICTORIAT
ITATVIVICTORIACAOOIRVIAOTVICTORIACO
CIVIIOCTITRORICOTVVOROAIAIOIOAVOCOA
CVICTORIATITOACORTVRICOOVVVOIAROAIR
IVICTORIAITITIIITRTRVVICTORIAIARVVI
OOARCCTCVRCRIITOIITROIARVICTORIAIVC
IATVICTORIAOTIOVATRITOIVRCTRRTOCTTV
```

Decrypted original text from the previous page:
COMMUNICATION

Mark and count: HANNAH

```
FKADEAVAJFGSSDVTBRYYHANNAHDTONJPFIV
TUBQDKYUHATFAMGBNPDNMTATGGISBMWTFJX
UUJAZFOECHPLWHHANNAHALNBGEYJMSHTPKU
XNUSBHANNAHKIXHANNAHGWKKDIOCIEVHXQF
HANNAHHRIHANNAHYSTRYQYFSHANNAHHREEN
EZQTDUKSKWNKHANNAHSXDFGHANNAHHPNMCP
GTRHSFHANNAHZFTCVAFAAPAYQFMSKCMXGLD
FGZYWITVGAHOFXAEMXMUHSADEYFILPQOUSQ
ESADIIFGZSYPPVWFDTPVHNNCBDBQWXSIKLC
FTGHSNFHUILSGVHANNAHVQHCDXFAMXNFZEE
XEBMIHHANNAHSPKDETKUNFUHHCHANNAHRQR
FUOLYZLLNWESERLZPBCRFNWGMHANNAHYPUS
IMIPVAELLYOBDFRXMIKGVXCGTCPBEXEJMPH
OJUSSTEQXQVGNEZDEBTTGWRRYWAXTZTZLCI
SDJSJGVFCJDSULCMWZNQFBSYHANNAHWXDPP
NGRRWKQQEOISDNKIUBXUTTKIOHWQHANNAHU
XETLSOIXKHANNAHFNPJJRHBXMGQZFQVEYEP
OWFPODJJLYHANNAHJCVNHANNAHUEHANNAHA
KHANNAHJJXUUWHNYPFSAWGOYASKICXNNEHL
CRZUMKVEEVMVUASLQCPBQSPIIHANNAHVDPU
UAKBHANNAHHANNAHQOVHANNAHDHANNAHNQE
FTPHXHEENQEDJWSRMLRIZUPUSTLEUPINLDY
NQGECEHANNAHRLFJANKWRYGTMHANNAHDOUW
FGGCPKHANNAHJGQNKRLGWCSGYMUYGGIAWFZ
YZZHANNAHKDTBMUOISOHHYHSYNEHANNAHRO
TRVSPKPDANYCXTKQLQTXMZFQJGWQETUUWQF
ZNAGWTRHSJEOATSHANNAHRAURVFWHANNAHZ
ALPCPWHANNAHDOHIZDPMFXCVMRSZOEZREPD
VXKWHANNAHVSJCIHANNAHCXHANNAHORVQBM
```

35	21
28	15
81	21
12	35
31	4
29	6
20	23
27	32
29	12
4	25
10	4
28	17
34	21
18	15
46	22
30	18
16	18
58	12
38	25
6	36

Are you sure? See page 194!

CALCULATE

2 • 8 = _____	2 • 4 = _____
14 - 6 = _____	28 - 12 = _____
16 + 2 = _____	23 - 9 = _____
9 + 8 = _____	24 - 8 = _____
12 - 9 = _____	25 - 14 = _____
14 - 3 = _____	21 + 9 = _____
2 • 10 = _____	4 + 4 = _____
6 + 11 = _____	29 - 13 = _____
19 - 13 = _____	10 • 4 = _____
16 - 16 = _____	6 • 5 = _____
9 • 2 = _____	19 + 11 = _____
2 + 3 = _____	16 + 5 = _____
7 - 7 = _____	21 - 9 = _____
15 - 14 = _____	13 - 13 = _____
8 + 2 = _____	20 + 4 = _____
4 • 6 = _____	17 - 6 = _____
3 + 11 = _____	23 - 14 = _____
2 • 3 = _____	3 • 3 = _____
17 - 11 = _____	14 - 12 = _____
2 • 7 = _____	4 • 10 = _____

Additional tasks - only for math lovers!

$5 \cdot 7 =$ ____	$3 \cdot 7 =$ ____
$19 + 9 =$ ____	$5 \cdot 3 =$ ____
$9 \cdot 9 =$ ____	$25 - 4 =$ ____
$6 \cdot 2 =$ ____	$7 \cdot 5 =$ ____
$23 + 8 =$ ____	$25 - 21 =$ ____
$34 - 5 =$ ____	$2 \cdot 3 =$ ____
$5 \cdot 4 =$ ____	$7 + 16 =$ ____
$3 \cdot 9 =$ ____	$8 \cdot 4 =$ ____
$40 - 11 =$ ____	$2 \cdot 6 =$ ____
$33 - 29 =$ ____	$15 + 10 =$ ____
$5 \cdot 2 =$ ____	$2 \cdot 2 =$ ____
$7 \cdot 4 =$ ____	$29 - 12 =$ ____
$27 + 7 =$ ____	$14 + 7 =$ ____
$6 \cdot 3 =$ ____	$4 + 11 =$ ____
$19 + 27 =$ ____	$13 + 9 =$ ____
$5 \cdot 6 =$ ____	$14 + 4 =$ ____
$8 \cdot 2 =$ ____	$7 + 11 =$ ____
$38 + 20 =$ ____	$15 - 3 =$ ____
$27 + 11 =$ ____	$4 + 21 =$ ____
$12 - 6 =$ ____	$9 \cdot 4 =$ ____

FIND THE NUMBERS!

16 8
8 16
18 14
17 16
3 11
11 30
20 8
17 16
6 40
0 30
18 30
5 21
0 12
1 0
10 24
24 11
14 9
6 9
6 2
14 40

Mark and count: 6

```
6 0 1 6 4 4 8 5 4 0 6 5 7 0 9 8 5 2
8 2 2 6 2 4 0 2 6 8 0 7 2 4 0 7 6 2
3 0 9 0 2 6 4 6 1 1 1 4 6 9 3 0 9 5
0 9 5 8 1 9 1 8 0 1 7 4 2 2 0 4 7 9
7 2 7 1 1 1 7 8 3 2 1 9 9 8 0 2 3 9
2 7 5 0 6 8 7 8 6 9 9 3 9 1 6 2 2 5
1 3 1 9 0 3 5 3 6 0 3 6 9 0 9 5 3 6
4 2 6 5 1 5 0 7 2 9 1 9 8 2 0 2 6 6
1 4 2 4 2 9 5 6 8 4 5 6 9 4 2 0 7 8
4 3 8 7 1 7 9 0 8 6 1 5 3 1 0 8 7 3
2 5 5 1 0 1 8 7 3 7 3 9 8 2 8 9 9 5
5 3 5 8 2 7 7 4 6 4 2 0 3 9 9 5 0 9
5 7 5 9 2 9 2 4 8 4 5 2 8 0 7 3 6 6
```

Mark and count: 28

```
75 76 63 69 83 28 77 94 28 28 98 16
58 78 35 34 42 32 58 31 76 44 28 90
75 28 17 52 28 27 62 36 68 21 66 93
29 99 28 69 91 59 71 12 91 49 80 25
13 84 16 86 55 97 54 84 24 71 27 42
74 28 74 78 32 88 28 77 12 95 31 13
52 62 33 69 92 39 72 39 21 65 71 21
15 72 69 56 32 28 14 24 33 57 28 29
16 83 43 90 30 37 27 28 28 36 25 81
65 70 92 12 87 17 61 80 91 82 63 38
69 68 29 11 83 28 89 49 95 28 18 13
32 88 29 33 28 58 78 46 88 87 64 83
28 88 12 15 28 97 51 62 43 26 50 81
```

Are you sure? See page 195!

Now make a simple sketch of the memorized picture with as many details as possible:

TRY TO REMEMBER!

What should you find?

- City: _____
- Name: _____
- Decrypted text: _____

day 8

WARM UP!

$3 + 6 =$ _____

$6 + 3 =$ _____

$3 - 2 =$ _____

$18 - 12 =$ _____

$6 + 5 =$ _____

$2 \cdot 10 =$ _____

$15 - 15 =$ _____

$6 \cdot 4 =$ _____

$6 + 11 =$ _____

$19 - 2 =$ _____

$2 \cdot 5 =$ _____

$18 - 4 =$ _____

$5 - 5 =$ _____

$11 - 10 =$ _____

$16 - 2 =$ _____

$8 \cdot 3 =$ _____

$3 \cdot 2 =$ _____

$2 + 12 =$ _____

$7 + 3 =$ _____

$7 \cdot 3 =$ _____

$14 + 16 =$ _____

$7 - 7 =$ _____

$4 + 24 =$ _____

$2 \cdot 9 =$ _____

$20 + 9 =$ _____

$5 \cdot 9 =$ _____

$14 - 3 =$ _____

$26 - 13 =$ _____

$17 + 11 =$ _____

$24 - 11 =$ _____

$7 \cdot 2 =$ _____

$4 \cdot 5 =$ _____

$3 \cdot 6 =$ _____

$6 + 7 =$ _____

$15 - 6 =$ _____

$3 \cdot 4 =$ _____

$5 + 23 =$ _____

$3 \cdot 3 =$ _____

$5 \cdot 2 =$ _____

$5 \cdot 8 =$ _____

Decipher the following code with the "Caesar encryption".

The required character offset to the right is: 2

G R Q Y L M R Y T C P W

_ _ _ _ _ _ _ _ _ _ _ _

Copy the decrypted text on page 197.

ABCDEFGHIJKLMNOPQRSTUVWXYZ_ABCDEF

Memorize this picture and all of its details as best as you can to make a sketch of it later.

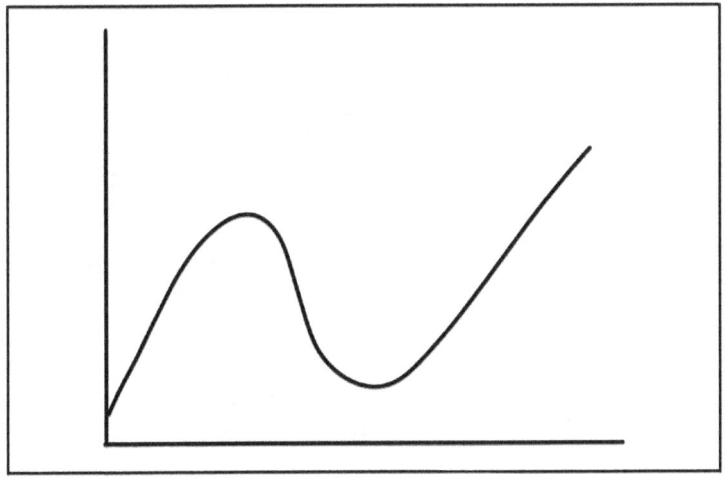

9	30
9	0
1	28
6	18
11	29
20	45
0	11
24	13
17	28
17	13
10	14
14	20
0	18
1	13
14	9
24	12
6	28
14	9
10	10
21	40

Mark and count: S

```
CCCCCCCCCCCCCCCCCCCCCCCCCCCCCCCCCCCCCC
CCCCCCCCCCCCCCCCCCCCCCCCCCCCCCSCCCCSSC
SCCCCCCCCCCCCCCCCCCCCCCCCCCCCCCCCCCCCS
CCCCCCCCCCCCCCCCCSCCCCCCCCCCCCCCCCCCCC
CCCCCCCCCCCCCCCCCSCCCCCCCCCCCCCCCCCCCC
CCCCCCCCCCCCCCCCCCCCCCCCCCCCCCCCCCCCCC
CCCCCCCCSCCCCCCSCCCCCSCCCCCSCSCCCCC
CCCCCCCCCCCCCCCCCCCCCSCCCCCCCSCCCC
CCCCCCCCCCCCCCCCCCCCCCCCCCCCCCCCCCCC
CCCCCCCCCCCCCCCCCCCCCCCCCCCCCSCCCC
CCCCCCCCCCCCCCCCCCCCCCCCCCCCCCCCCCCCC
CCCCCCCCCCCSCCCCCCCCCCCCCCCCCCCSCC
CCCCCCCCCCSSCCCCCCCCCCCCCCCCCCCCCCC
```

Mark and count: TOKYO

```
OOYTOKYOOOOYOYTOOOTOKYOKYKOTOKTOTTO
OOOOYKYKOOOTOOOKOKOOYKOKOOOOYKTOYTO
OTOKYOOOOYYOOOKYOYKTYTYTTOKYOYKOTKO
YKKTTOTYTOKYOYKOTYOOOKOOOOOKOOTYOYO
YYTOKYOTKOOYTOKOTYOTOKYOYKOKOYYTYKY
YKOTTYKYKKKOOOOOYTOKYOYYOOTTKYOOOTT
KTOYKYYTOKYOOOOYTOKYOTOKYOKYOTTOYTY
OYYYOOTTOKYOOYTTTTOKYOKTKOOOKOOOTOT
YKOKOYTTOKTOKYOKOYTOOOTTYTOKYOOTOTO
TOKTOKYOTTYYKYOYTOKYOYTTYKYTOKYOTOY
TYKOYKKOTOKYOOOTYTYOYOKOKKYOKYOYYKY
OYTTOOTOKYOKYTTOTOOKOOOOOYTKYTOYOOO
KOOOYKKYKYYOOYKKYOOOYKTTOKYOYYTOKOO
```

88

Decrypted original text from the previous page:
ITS NOT VERY

Mark and count: THOMAS

```
RJHFTHOMASTXXXDYYHTYLCYCTHOMASLSUMA
ADERTHOMASRLRPZDJKZWVLJPTHOMASPEUSG
THOMASMTTHOMASTHOMASRFNRCMYJHLMPWNF
MIRYLZTHOMASHYTUAFIDHATHOMASUUNYSTX
FKVCFWEYHUJTWBUTHOMASTJTBTLHNCTRTRS
ZGCZATHOMASEAAZEGNPLMWDBIOTFPIQWJDR
BPCWESUILUBNBUNYZFXOZQKXTHOMASVCJUX
RLVQEHMXSTHOMASGQPOUPJGKIETHOMASKVV
HLSDUJXILGYQEKFJSIORBFSIHQRKWYUZWNZ
GDHFFHAFRYORTZVLUFITIRCNAJPCRKIOAJX
XLTTHOMASFJMPAMTHOMASGWRFCUGYQGYMAJ
RVDFDTHOMASITHOMASHTJGAPJTHOMASJNYJ
KHTHOMASATHOMASLIBWSYMIBSODCSWSAOLG
IZXNEVHZKGVRWTHOMASVGQKHLDJVTHOMASO
LOKNQFQWDLSRHFHLYWYTCJYQIHSXRRXJDAX
ELBMCXRIFVSATAWTHOMASMKTLMTHOMASGZF
JBXOZJJTHOMASETAOKLPPMBLLLYZWCAWYNG
MEEPTQVRYEFDACIVCJTHOMASAMLLKVAVJYZ
BRQTHOMASUSFRLFNJXUQBPJVBNXUUTGPJCT
DELHDOPLTHOMASSKBVPRNLLODSJNTHOMASF
GKTHOMASUPOCZVZCTHOMASJBHRTHOMASZYY
RFTQPALIMQDCKWVDHIUQATITHOMASXQWKVN
XUIEXCZTTPTHOMASXOBGZHOTHOMASUCJPNN
NXKUTHOMASKTHOMASNGLSKKICDWQLRDRDTR
YWERWNFVTHSNUVQEBTHOMASOANRDURMUOSL
NQCMQRVIHZZDAQMBMASDSZDPPINJEBMIJYH
DCSPSCXLFPFWDOOQRDOAFYMKBAGGATHOMAS
JSDAZSPQSYEXSHVQWFWRTLFQQSOQUUDARCI
ZTHOMASDBUSUHMFXTHOMASRUJHTHOMASSIU
```

32	40
52	40
6	12
32	18
25	29
40	20
16	32
24	30
20	14
38	2
37	28
10	12
38	20
28	14
48	15
39	35
43	14
13	16
25	15
46	18

Are you sure? See page 194!

CALCULATE

3 + 7 = _____	4 + 22 = _____
3 · 4 = _____	18 + 5 = _____
9 + 11 = _____	11 - 8 = _____
4 · 2 = _____	18 + 12 = _____
5 + 4 = _____	7 - 5 = _____
4 + 13 = _____	17 + 8 = _____
2 + 8 = _____	14 + 4 = _____
2 · 2 = _____	12 + 11 = _____
3 · 8 = _____	12 - 9 = _____
3 · 5 = _____	22 - 16 = _____
16 + 3 = _____	26 - 3 = _____
10 · 2 = _____	11 + 4 = _____
9 + 8 = _____	13 - 13 = _____
16 - 5 = _____	2 · 9 = _____
12 - 3 = _____	11 + 5 = _____
5 + 6 = _____	17 - 5 = _____
15 - 7 = _____	5 · 2 = _____
12 + 8 = _____	4 + 18 = _____
5 · 4 = _____	13 + 7 = _____
7 - 3 = _____	2 · 5 = _____

day 8

Additional tasks - only for math lovers!

21 + 11 = ____	10 • 4 = ____
22 + 30 = ____	8 • 5 = ____
3 • 2 = ____	15 - 3 = ____
4 • 8 = ____	5 + 13 = ____
45 - 20 = ____	7 + 22 = ____
5 • 8 = ____	6 + 14 = ____
2 • 8 = ____	8 • 4 = ____
4 • 6 = ____	6 • 5 = ____
4 • 5 = ____	2 • 7 = ____
43 - 5 = ____	26 - 24 = ____
46 - 9 = ____	7 • 4 = ____
40 - 30 = ____	6 • 2 = ____
47 - 9 = ____	10 • 2 = ____
40 - 12 = ____	10 + 4 = ____
8 • 6 = ____	3 • 5 = ____
8 + 31 = ____	5 • 7 = ____
17 + 26 = ____	7 • 2 = ____
18 - 5 = ____	27 - 11 = ____
5 • 5 = ____	26 - 11 = ____
16 + 30 = ____	6 • 3 = ____

FIND THE NUMBERS!

10 26

12 23

20 3

8 30

9 2

17 25

10 18

4 23

24 3

15 6

19 23

20 15

17 0

11 18

9 16

11 12

8 10

20 22

20 20

4 10

Mark and count: 9

```
5 9 6 5 3 6 0 2 3 6 9 7 2 0 0 1 3 1
0 2 0 7 2 8 5 8 2 5 7 6 4 0 8 8 0 5
1 6 4 9 1 3 4 0 1 3 8 9 6 9 4 4 6 5
5 3 9 8 2 3 4 6 1 7 0 9 7 9 2 2 1 6
5 6 4 0 6 1 5 4 3 0 8 8 1 8 4 7 9 0
9 8 0 6 1 7 0 7 7 0 6 0 6 5 9 3 3 7
1 8 1 4 9 4 2 0 4 6 0 5 9 8 7 7 4 9
1 5 1 3 8 2 5 1 1 7 7 1 6 9 2 8 0 2
0 9 3 7 8 3 2 3 3 2 3 2 2 9 9 9 5 4
6 2 6 3 9 7 5 0 4 3 1 5 8 3 3 1 6 0
2 0 9 2 2 3 5 7 3 0 8 3 0 7 4 8 2 9
2 2 7 9 2 6 6 8 3 7 8 3 4 9 2 3 9 3
3 9 6 7 7 3 6 5 9 8 6 8 4 1 9 4 9 1
```

Mark and count: 97

```
11 94 55 36 12 52 24 14 78 47 41 42
97 35 80 10 88 72 29 21 51 86 87 26
31 49 33 62 70 81 51 75 82 50 14 92
91 90 49 97 97 14 93 78 52 18 97 16
66 97 93 85 97 36 97 40 72 97 93 92
97 97 15 77 36 73 54 73 47 47 61 35
40 52 63 17 71 52 18 73 43 43 84 48
97 55 88 66 74 45 54 40 43 43 80 43
34 48 51 14 36 77 31 78 38 42 91 35
50 21 78 55 75 19 30 83 89 48 68 79
52 17 68 53 20 71 66 31 27 21 65 12
80 85 11 70 34 65 64 97 73 86 15 68
80 35 17 75 14 79 65 61 52 98 97 97
```

Are you sure? See page 195!

Now make a simple sketch of the memorized picture
with as many details as possible:

TRY TO REMEMBER!

What should you find?

- City: _____
- Name: _____
- Decrypted text: _____

day 9

WARM UP!

2 • 5 = _____	2 • 9 = _____
7 + 5 = _____	5 • 2 = _____
19 - 15 = _____	17 - 6 = _____
19 - 9 = _____	22 + 7 = _____
9 + 11 = _____	21 - 11 = _____
12 + 6 = _____	8 • 6 = _____
3 • 6 = _____	3 • 4 = _____
5 • 3 = _____	9 • 5 = _____
4 • 3 = _____	23 - 15 = _____
7 - 2 = _____	25 - 9 = _____
16 - 11 = _____	11 + 6 = _____
14 - 9 = _____	14 - 5 = _____
16 - 8 = _____	7 • 5 = _____
7 - 4 = _____	29 - 16 = _____
19 - 4 = _____	9 • 3 = _____
13 + 2 = _____	9 + 6 = _____
4 + 13 = _____	13 + 13 = _____
17 - 14 = _____	19 - 7 = _____
7 + 10 = _____	28 - 25 = _____
20 - 10 = _____	10 + 7 = _____

Decipher the following code with the "Caesar encryption".

The required character offset to the right is: 5

N _ Y P M _ V X P O

_ _ _ _ _ _ _ _ _ _

Copy the decrypted text on page 197.

ABCDEFGHIJKLMNOPQRSTUVWXYZ_ABCDEF

Memorize this picture and all of its details as best as you can to make a sketch of it later.

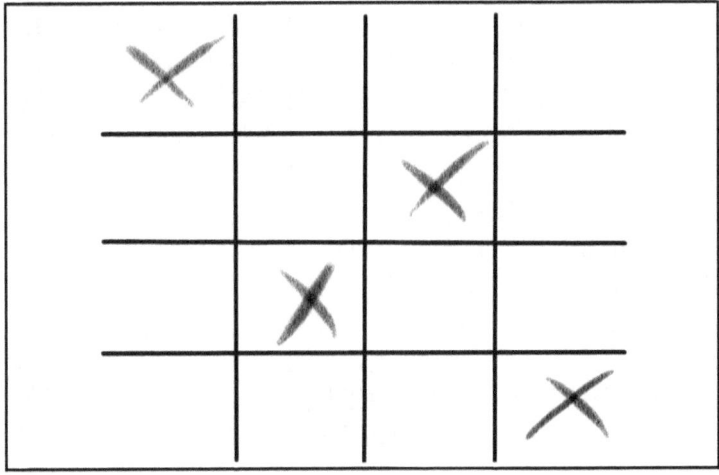

WORDS AND LETTERS

10 18
12 10
4 11
10 29
20 10
18 48
18 12
15 45
12 8
5 16
5 17
5 9
8 35
3 13
15 27
15 15
17 26
3 12
17 3
10 17

Mark and count: A

```
VVVVVVVVVAVVVVVVVVVVVAVVVVVVVVVVVV
VVVVVVVVVVVVVVAVVVVVVVVVVVVVVVVVVV
VVVVVVVVVVVVVVVVVVVVVVVVVVVAVVVVVV
VVVVVAVVVVVVVVVVVVVVVVVVVVVVVVVVVV
VVVVVVVVVVVAVAVVVVVVVVVVVVVVVVVVVV
VVVVVVVVAVVVVVVVVVVVVVVVVVVVVVVVVV
VVVVVVVVVVVVVVVVVVVVVVVVVVVVVVVVVV
VVVVVVVVVVVVVVVVVVVVVVVVVVVVVVVVVV
VAVVVVVVVVVVVVVVVVVVVVVVVAVAVVAVVV
VVVVVVVVVAVVVVVVVVVVVAVVVVVVVVVVVV
VVVAVVAVVVVVAVVVVVAVVVVVVVVVVVAVV
VVVVVVVVVVVVVVVVVVVVVVVVAVVVVVVVVV
VAVVVVVAVVVVVVVVVAVVVVVVVVAVVVVVVV
```

Mark and count: SEOUL

```
OUUSEOULLSLUSEOULSLEOLSSEOULOEOSSEL
ESOEUUSSEOUUSUOEESEOULEOSLSOOOLUUOL
EOOLSEOULSLUOLOUEUESLUULUELLEESOSOE
OOOOLUSOSEOULOLOEESUOLESSSUUOLULEEE
EOESSEUUSLESEOULOSEUSSOOSEOULUSEOUL
ULOSEOEUEEOSSLEOUEUUOUUULLOSSSEOULU
EUEUSEUEUUOOELSEOULSOLLEEOEOOUSOOOE
SSSLUOSSOLUOSSUUOUOEUOOUSEOULLUEELO
OLLSEOULSLLSLULSOLUUUOOLEULUEELOESS
LOOSOLLEOUESOSEEESEOULSESEOULOLESLE
LSEOULSEOULSELOLOSLOSEOULSLSOULOLES
OEEOOEOOLOOSLLLSSESEOULOLSSEOEEEUSL
EESSOSEOULSEOULLUOSEOULSEOULULSELOS
```

Decrypted original text from the previous page:
SECURE BUT

98

Mark and count: JAMES

```
VOLESYHYAWTGOTVYQIPGPUPFLJAMESONTAE
ZQAIJMCVYZEXXMQFDILNPWMEEJFWNJLDGDB
EVOMMBNTMXWMTYETIIPDKYWPGUJAMESDHHF
OJYNAECKGECSRQZQVBRAJAMESZDLHNYLEQZ
HVBDKPEBOZJAMESDPYLMXJAMESXBXEOBOKI
NVFKGMZCXENHVUJAMESNUJAMESGFWHPFDZP
TWXNHAZQLUKRONXMZWLUOHFBPSSCXJAMESO
UPWUTBXUNKWPOHAJXMLXTJIYWWDOQNAULBP
WJYGGAKGTJAEUPUSPIWYHSMZZRIPSMSOQKK
UNPDJXSXCWBWZXAALLWLRAUAVAITUGAJDTM
HIDYKTDJAMESNBFWMLNQZBTTIEJAMESDZTE
UZWESADDBPGBBHARXMRAEZIYGJAMESZINEN
DUBZWMLBZJEEGKTMVFGJAMESKHSLEPSNXFO
WIRAGUALTCNKDCWQJLJEORRUPHJPURECBJB
LDKFFFNUDEHCRBJAMESZITVBBVZUHBAFTJV
SNUUSPNRIRJAMESYRANGNXGSUHLCFKYYQZR
ZLPZWILSVZIJHSAJAMESYWJBNAQCFRTHQOL
BJAMESWYCOMZJILZYLWJAMESYYMJAMESYLJ
KQTYSPGXIFDIAZHBHXKEPQSWBOSMRBIMNWU
CFQIBPTVKJLNDILIKHRZILCATTWVXTBJPUJ
LWTFTZSVEQTUXNMJIHTDEOJAMESZUCPOTPC
OHNJAMESSLOCLRJGQXJAMESHIQJBJAMESKD
SLJAMESMNEHLLOSLIYJAMESHRJAMESVMVLV
YJTROTHSXFDPOEQDUBIGLNWVDGVDOEAZBEM
FKCNFITFJOLPYYXJAMESENBQEALIOWYSFFF
QXZBLJLRFMUKMSOXKPUDXEORGUATTXSARXP
FUTJAMESUPDXYHBWRNRXKVJSLBAAMQAQVJP
SNJAMESZMPTOPTAHTJAMESHSJCXGYUJAMES
YJAMESUJCVQLSJITPMPHSSRJAMESJAMESTV
```

12	22
18	18
33	48
58	5
10	18
38	15
22	18
20	8
45	27
21	35
10	4
46	18
56	6
3	21
56	18
42	4
14	21
80	1
48	20
35	9

Are you sure? See page 194!

CALCULATE

12 - 3 = ____	9 + 10 = ____
10 + 6 = ____	10 • 3 = ____
17 - 14 = ____	21 + 5 = ____
4 • 3 = ____	18 + 7 = ____
6 • 4 = ____	2 • 10 = ____
11 + 4 = ____	12 + 13 = ____
5 + 2 = ____	21 - 10 = ____
20 - 20 = ____	2 • 8 = ____
3 + 3 = ____	6 • 8 = ____
9 - 6 = ____	30 - 5 = ____
15 + 4 = ____	6 + 6 = ____
4 • 4 = ____	13 + 17 = ____
9 + 7 = ____	23 - 11 = ____
7 + 6 = ____	8 - 8 = ____
4 • 5 = ____	5 + 13 = ____
2 • 3 = ____	19 + 8 = ____
18 - 14 = ____	28 - 21 = ____
7 + 7 = ____	22 - 18 = ____
9 • 2 = ____	13 + 7 = ____
2 + 8 = ____	9 + 6 = ____

Additional tasks - only for math lovers!

2 • 6 = _____	29 - 7 = _____
26 - 8 = _____	6 • 3 = _____
47 - 14 = _____	8 • 6 = _____
31 + 27 = _____	17 - 12 = _____
5 • 2 = _____	8 + 10 = _____
30 + 8 = _____	18 - 3 = _____
45 - 23 = _____	3 • 6 = _____
50 - 30 = _____	15 - 7 = _____
9 • 5 = _____	3 • 9 = _____
48 - 27 = _____	5 • 7 = _____
43 - 33 = _____	23 - 19 = _____
14 + 32 = _____	2 • 9 = _____
32 + 24 = _____	17 - 11 = _____
29 - 26 = _____	25 - 4 = _____
7 • 8 = _____	9 • 2 = _____
7 • 6 = _____	30 - 26 = _____
2 • 7 = _____	12 + 9 = _____
10 • 8 = _____	18 - 17 = _____
21 + 27 = _____	4 • 5 = _____
19 + 16 = _____	29 - 20 = _____

9	19
16	30
3	26
12	25
24	20
15	25
7	11
0	16
6	48
3	25
19	12
16	30
16	12
13	0
20	18
6	27
4	7
14	4
18	20
10	15

Mark and count: 5

```
2 4 0 3 5 4 8 1 9 6 6 4 7 1 3 7 2 1
8 0 8 7 4 4 5 2 9 7 0 7 8 6 4 1 1 8
1 8 9 4 7 9 2 2 9 2 7 0 8 0 9 5 7 3
1 0 0 1 8 7 5 5 8 4 0 8 0 0 1 2 0 5
4 6 9 0 5 7 6 6 0 9 0 1 7 5 2 8 3 3
8 0 4 4 9 7 2 8 3 3 0 3 1 8 5 5 3 1
1 6 3 6 9 7 8 4 2 4 4 1 9 9 5 8 8 3
5 8 1 9 6 9 8 5 5 4 8 5 4 9 3 9 2 1
3 0 2 9 3 3 6 4 5 9 6 9 9 0 8 8 9 6
5 4 8 0 2 4 2 3 9 8 6 7 6 9 9 5 4 3
0 3 0 9 6 1 3 7 6 7 5 9 7 0 8 7 8 4
1 5 5 2 0 6 3 3 1 1 4 6 3 1 9 2 0 7
8 5 5 0 7 9 0 9 3 4 4 6 1 1 6 3 2 7
```

Mark and count: 56

```
28 74 27 54 63 57 74 45 34 39 35 85
87 72 32 69 18 99 92 51 67 99 14 55
67 47 56 66 99 91 56 21 89 11 97 95
65 34 50 27 26 62 60 80 82 28 72 56
63 89 66 38 31 71 56 64 74 37 21 56
48 56 93 66 27 76 99 58 68 24 19 17
79 20 11 12 61 96 68 30 56 85 75 87
75 13 52 37 43 55 22 19 62 37 57 18
21 25 59 81 69 19 77 56 78 18 44 11
53 27 63 88 83 91 73 84 60 34 82 91
75 97 17 23 59 13 56 10 52 19 56 37
13 39 46 90 89 13 26 56 41 79 18 76
49 47 15 56 19 51 38 13 38 15 28 97
```

 Are you sure? See page 195!

Now make a simple sketch of the memorized picture
with as many details as possible:

TRY TO REMEMBER!

What should you find?

- City: _____
- Name: _____
- Decrypted text: _____

day 10

WARM UP!

$13 + 4 =$ _____ $22 - 5 =$ _____

$8 \cdot 2 =$ _____ $6 + 23 =$ _____

$9 + 8 =$ _____ $2 \cdot 3 =$ _____

$15 - 12 =$ _____ $8 + 21 =$ _____

$8 + 3 =$ _____ $17 + 13 =$ _____

$4 + 10 =$ _____ $24 - 5 =$ _____

$20 - 4 =$ _____ $25 - 16 =$ _____

$6 \cdot 2 =$ _____ $15 - 8 =$ _____

$3 \cdot 8 =$ _____ $7 \cdot 4 =$ _____

$3 \cdot 5 =$ _____ $25 - 21 =$ _____

$10 + 5 =$ _____ $8 \cdot 5 =$ _____

$7 \cdot 3 =$ _____ $5 \cdot 2 =$ _____

$17 - 7 =$ _____ $25 - 18 =$ _____

$18 - 4 =$ _____ $17 - 16 =$ _____

$6 + 2 =$ _____ $10 \cdot 4 =$ _____

$20 - 13 =$ _____ $5 + 21 =$ _____

$16 - 5 =$ _____ $3 \cdot 4 =$ _____

$18 - 5 =$ _____ $16 - 7 =$ _____

$3 \cdot 2 =$ _____ $9 + 9 =$ _____

$4 + 13 =$ _____ $26 - 7 =$ _____

Decipher the following code with the "Caesar encryption".

The required character offset to the right is: 1

S V N Z S G N T R _ M C

_ _ _ _ _ _ _ _ _ _ _ _

Copy the decrypted text on page 197.

ABCDEFGHIJKLMNOPQRSTUVWXYZ_ABCDEF

Memorize this picture and all of its details as best as you can to make a sketch of it later.

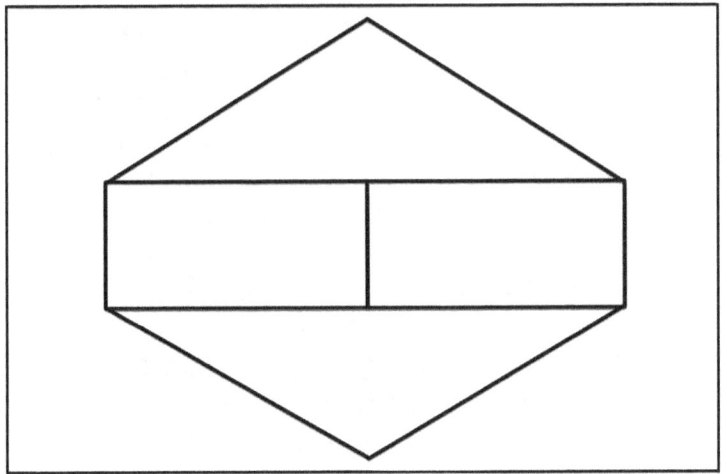

17	17
16	29
17	6
3	29
11	30
14	19
16	9
12	7
24	28
15	4
15	40
21	10
10	7
14	1
8	40
7	26
11	12
13	9
6	18
17	19

Mark and count: H

```
KKKKKKKKKKKHKKKKKKKKKKKKKHKKHKKHKKKK
KKKKKKKKKKKKKKKKKKKKKKKKKKKKKKKKKKKKK
KKKKKKKKKKKKKKKKKKKKKKKKKHKHKKKKKKH
KKKKKHKKKHKKKKKKKKKKKKHKKKKKKKKKKKKK
KHKKKKKKKKKKHKKKKKHKKKKKKKKKKKKKKKKK
KKKKKKKKKKKKKKKHKKKKKKKKKKKKHKKKKKH
KKKKKKKKKKKKKKKKKKKKKKKKKKKKKKKKKKKKK
KKKKKKHKKHKKKKKKKKKKKKKKKKKKKKKKKKKK
KKKKKKKKKKKKKKKKKHKKKKKKKKKKKKKKKKKK
KKKKKKKKKKKKKKKHKKKKKKKKKKKKKKKKKKKK
KKKKKKKKKKKKKKKKKKKKKKKKKKKKKKKKKKKKK
KKKKKKKKKKKKKKKKKHKKKKKKKKKKKKKKKKKK
KKKKKKKKKKKKKKKKKKKKKKKKKKKKKKKKKKKKK
```

Mark and count: SEATTLE

```
EELTTETLTESEATTLESEATTLETTTSEATTLES
ATTLEETETLSTTETEEESEETTLTETSATEEET
TLTSSSSTESALSATTEEESASLTTTTTELLSSET
SAEEETSLTEETATSLALASETSEATTLETAELLS
EESEATTLETTTAEEEESETLTTEAETSEATTLEE
ATELTTSTAESEATTLETSLESLEELTTSEATTLE
SEATTLETTTEELLETESTSEATTLEALLTETEEE
EEAESEATTLEETATTEESSSALLTESEASTTEET
LSLAAETETTSESALLSEATTLEATSLLATTTTLE
LELSSEATTLEELLTLAETEETAEEETSAEATELE
TTEESSEETEELTAATLELTAATESEATTLEELTA
ELTTEEEALATTSEEEESLTSSEETATALTTLLAS
SEEESTELEESEATTLETSEATTLEAEETETSETL
```

Decrypted original text from the previous page:
TWO THOUSAND

Mark and count: EMILY

```
PXEMILYLBIOQPHKROWEMILYFXLQNJMJLPEC
ZTHEHAPEMILYFAJPNHLASDEEMILYXNHXPFN
IADKQUVDTXESNEUVVFXXTREEZHKBBIILMCF
UAYFYXPEGPFIQVIJSAGEMILYGAEMILYBKXH
MWCVXEMILYUWCQUEMILYYRVEMILYTVKOWFT
VNEYNVOYWVCZXCZMCAREEMILYREMILYKYHR
EMILYRFSBXZHPZAVXTNYLXEMILYEHXAMDIL
WQNIEZZKCWPCIJZBCPTCOUAEMILYNTZIYVD
PEMILYYIZWUKZPQKNIUZKQVQYJEBGZWDHXE
AEMILYADPQRYWEEMILYZEMILYTTEMILYLCJ
RMJFUJHALSAEMILYXMRCDESQDIJNEMILYER
XLSTDBVAIMEMILYDPDMMAAAAVXVEEMILYDM
PDHMBFBLMUXXFCMUZSMEMILYLHTVZSEKEEY
AIDMEEMILYIXAHOHEGIQCRLRENSPJMZVNXV
EMILYAJXHPSBVLVJEOEMILYFIWRCIEMILYK
TWPQLECUHNEMILYCRRIAFIRRPEMILYEMILY
CGFLQRTKGJJZCINKGKPYEMILYFVYOGUILHW
GSMSZVPUMKOTEMILYLRXSPDTFZLZFBHGSNK
EMILYWUPMYHTINFDWTAGEMILYHONDRJGKIJ
NOBCWBVJQTZKMOBLOEBDCFKMEMILYXMEFDZ
AUWANEMILYDGQEQIPBNLOBVDZACXXTNSDHG
SOXXWBFHOHOFKREMILYEMILYTDNXERRSHTG
FWNXNKRGMAEMILYEHUKVGTUFHHEMILYKQNJ
RXIUKLKDDJAZQTCONVNYHOENOJKVAWSARTR
NZGSONCBJWHYYUFTXZTJDOUPDTQDEMILYOP
XQSCCPESKFAWEJCAXGNLHUKYPXKJEMILYFK
XQHHIEMILYNXVZYTFGWEQKLWEMILYQCBGFS
GHEMILYDOGHACQRQANURWQCVKEHDHCTYTTT
NLDELLYTHPHXWJFWWLZTHALUGMHEJIBKFHB
```

23	36
9	28
32	12
37	24
43	20
13	40
53	48
25	29
1	21
16	4
80	29
12	28
6	7
39	6
18	8
45	2
12	20
52	36
6	19
28	4

Are you sure? See page 194!

CALCULATE

9 + 7 = ____	5 • 2 = ____
16 - 9 = ____	11 - 11 = ____
7 + 8 = ____	17 - 16 = ____
4 + 2 = ____	7 • 3 = ____
7 • 2 = ____	8 • 2 = ____
5 + 12 = ____	10 • 3 = ____
15 + 4 = ____	2 • 9 = ____
6 + 12 = ____	13 - 13 = ____
8 • 3 = ____	19 - 15 = ____
7 + 6 = ____	4 + 9 = ____
11 + 9 = ____	5 • 8 = ____
12 + 5 = ____	18 - 5 = ____
5 • 4 = ____	19 - 9 = ____
5 + 13 = ____	7 • 6 = ____
2 • 7 = ____	13 + 6 = ____
11 - 9 = ____	13 + 8 = ____
6 + 9 = ____	10 • 4 = ____
3 • 4 = ____	21 - 7 = ____
11 + 2 = ____	3 • 7 = ____
2 • 8 = ____	11 + 14 = ____

Additional tasks - only for math lovers!

49 - 26 = _____	4 • 9 = _____
3 • 3 = _____	7 • 4 = _____
49 - 17 = _____	2 • 6 = _____
11 + 26 = _____	5 + 19 = _____
50 - 7 = _____	10 • 2 = _____
34 - 21 = _____	8 • 5 = _____
16 + 37 = _____	8 • 6 = _____
5 • 5 = _____	18 + 11 = _____
42 - 41 = _____	17 + 4 = _____
27 - 11 = _____	15 - 11 = _____
8 • 10 = _____	10 + 19 = _____
4 • 3 = _____	4 • 7 = _____
3 • 2 = _____	17 - 10 = _____
11 + 28 = _____	23 - 17 = _____
38 - 20 = _____	23 - 15 = _____
12 + 33 = _____	18 - 16 = _____
26 - 14 = _____	13 + 7 = _____
19 + 33 = _____	6 • 6 = _____
2 • 3 = _____	9 + 10 = _____
36 - 8 = _____	12 - 8 = _____

FIND THE NUMBERS!

16	10
7	0
15	1
6	21
14	16
17	30
19	18
18	0
24	4
13	13
20	40
17	13
20	10
18	42
14	19
2	21
15	40
12	14
13	21
16	25

Mark and count: 3

```
3 4 2 4 2 7 3 9 2 1 0 1 9 6 8 0 8 8
9 7 8 0 2 0 1 7 0 9 0 0 5 9 8 3 0 2
9 7 8 3 7 0 6 6 0 9 7 0 8 6 5 2 5 2
8 9 4 2 0 8 9 1 2 6 5 4 7 4 9 6 9 6
6 7 5 4 7 3 4 2 3 8 1 8 2 3 1 5 7 3
6 8 1 9 9 0 5 4 7 9 9 9 2 4 6 5 0 4
3 2 1 6 4 2 8 3 7 8 4 0 2 3 3 4 6 3
8 0 1 7 4 6 4 4 0 9 5 8 6 8 6 3 9 3
9 3 7 8 9 1 2 2 0 3 8 5 0 7 6 8 4 8
1 4 1 7 3 0 8 3 9 2 6 2 6 3 6 5 6 9
6 6 9 8 5 7 0 1 0 5 9 0 5 1 9 1 8 1
5 4 8 7 0 6 0 4 4 9 1 2 5 9 8 7 4 9
4 7 2 2 7 0 0 5 8 6 6 6 1 1 1 6 5 1
```

Mark and count: 37

```
21 37 40 44 76 31 45 74 12 35 31 97
89 42 45 37 33 37 70 59 94 21 85 48
89 99 38 71 20 15 60 43 37 18 70 53
88 25 84 71 37 39 39 80 72 42 90 79
86 30 74 20 37 27 34 35 49 58 11 59
16 88 34 17 57 89 20 96 32 80 65 81
55 21 16 77 86 12 27 43 46 24 52 32
15 57 69 87 37 37 37 78 55 20 82 10
55 31 99 20 37 16 43 89 97 95 96 66
13 26 46 50 74 23 13 62 65 85 37 69
66 31 61 90 69 30 57 74 25 49 21 81
59 22 93 12 67 99 26 96 29 86 44 57
59 32 19 51 20 29 50 26 76 19 10 77
```

112

Are you sure? See page 195!

Now make a simple sketch of the memorized picture with as many details as possible:

```



```

TRY TO REMEMBER!

What should you find?

- City: _____
- Name: _____
- Decrypted text: _____

day 11

WARM UP!

5 + 8 = _____	11 + 12 = _____
10 + 8 = _____	9 + 6 = _____
3 • 5 = _____	4 • 8 = _____
11 − 2 = _____	7 − 6 = _____
13 + 4 = _____	19 − 6 = _____
10 − 2 = _____	6 • 8 = _____
11 + 8 = _____	9 • 5 = _____
11 − 9 = _____	2 • 5 = _____
8 + 11 = _____	2 • 7 = _____
7 + 4 = _____	4 • 2 = _____
16 − 7 = _____	9 + 9 = _____
3 + 4 = _____	8 • 4 = _____
20 − 9 = _____	2 • 9 = _____
8 + 12 = _____	14 − 11 = _____
6 + 14 = _____	11 − 8 = _____
8 • 3 = _____	4 • 3 = _____
2 • 10 = _____	15 − 7 = _____
3 − 3 = _____	6 + 16 = _____
4 • 5 = _____	3 • 9 = _____
11 + 9 = _____	4 + 13 = _____

Decipher the following code with the "Caesar encryption".

The required character offset to the right is: 6

S Z V L M U V A I U C N U Q V M

_ _ _ _ _ _ _ _ _ _ _ _ _ _ _ _

Copy the decrypted text on page 197.

ABCDEFGHIJKLMNOPQRSTUVWXYZ_ABCDEF

Memorize this picture and all of its details as best as you can to make a sketch of it later.

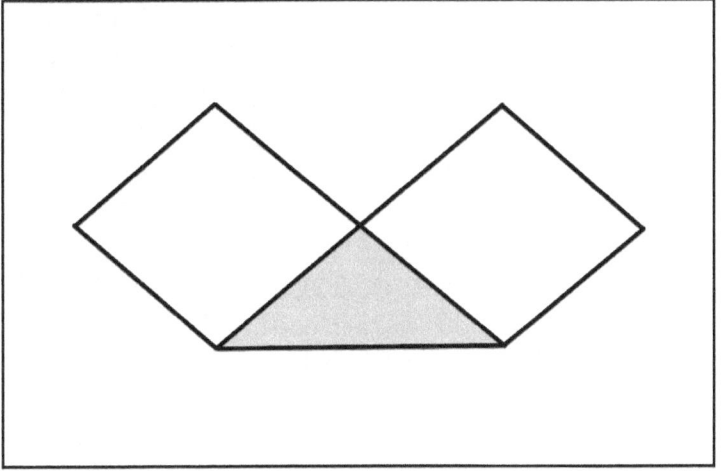

WORDS AND LETTERS

13	23
18	15
15	32
9	1
17	13
8	48
19	45
2	10
19	14
11	8
9	18
7	32
11	18
20	3
20	3
24	12
20	8
0	22
20	27
20	17

Mark and count: F

```
FHHHHHHHHHHHHHHHHHHHHHHHHHHHHHHHHHH
HHHHHHHHHHHHHHHHHHHHHHHHHHHHHHHHHHH
HHFHHHFHHHHHHHHHHHHHHHHHHHHHHHHHHHH
HHFHHHHHHHHHHHHHHHHHHHHHHHHHHHHHHHH
FHFHHHHFHHHHHHHHHHHHHHHHHHHHHHHHHHH
HHHFHHFHHHHHHHHHHHHHHHFHHHHHHHHHHHH
HHHHHHHHHHHHHHHHHHHHHHHHHHHHHHHHHHF
HHHHHHHHHHHHHHHHHHHHHHHHHHHHHHHHHHH
HHHHHHHHHHHHHHHHHHHHHHHHHFHHHHHHHHH
HHHHHHHHHHHHHHHHHHHHHHHHHHHHHHHHHHF
HHHHHHHHHHHHHHHHHHHHHHHHHHHHHHHHHHH
HHHHHHHHHHHHHHHHHHHHHHHHHHHHHHHHHHF
HHHHHHHFHHHHHHHHHHHHHHHFHHFHHHHFHHHHFHHHFH
```

Mark and count: OSLO

```
OLOOLLOLOOOOOOOOOLOOSSOSLOOSOOOSOOL
SOLSOLOLSOOOOSSSOLSSOSLOSSLOOOSLOOO
OSSOSSOOSLOLOOSLSSSLOOOOOSLOSOSLOSL
OSLSOOSOSLOSSLSSOOOOOOOSOOLOLLLOOOO
SLOSOLOOOOSOLOSLOSLSSLOOOLOSOLSLOLS
OOSLOSOSSOOSLOOSLOSOOOSLOLSOSSOSLOO
OOSLOOOOSLOOLOLOOOOSOSOSLOOSLOOSOOS
OSOOOSOSLOOOLOOOSSOSOOSLOOOOSSLSOOL
SOLOOLSOLSLLSOSLOLOOLLLSOSSOOLOSLLO
SOSLOOOOOLLLOOOOOSOSLOLLOSOLSOLSLSL
OSSLSOOLSOOOLOOOSLOLLOSOSLOLLLSLLSO
OSLOOLOSLOOOSLOOOSLOSLOLSOOOLOSOLSL
LOOLSOSLOSLOOSLOSOSLOOOOOLOSSLLOOSS
```

Decrypted original text from the previous page:
YEARS AGO IT WAS

118

Mark and count: MIA

```
CMXAMIAOOQJTWGFSSPMIAMFPAEQSTMIAHZJ
WTAYQEWURNUKORZCGHGRGCMUTHOYELTIDBN
ALLUPSFUGAVJOYRXPMNDJHHEGHNNLZKWEKP
PXEBBYVLABAYPFNOPZZDCIXVMIADGPPLZTF
MFHIIRPPBZWCMOXWMIASDVXVYODKUDZRZDD
MIAUXIYNEMIARMVHYPLWMIAOUMKMIAGQHCE
ASLIOICEZTRJNFEKTGILHLFGITBLRUXHYTJ
IMIAIRJJBYXLSPSVBRNYNEUIIMIALZOJMIA
CPKQFMKNVBEQPEJSRAMHTHIUMIAXXWPTQGI
HTVOENJBZOOMIANACNDSGYBTBWXNLPOQDMJ
XAJUZDGXWSRGRXTMOGCMIARQZVMIAHSZCLN
XNEOCLSBQJVCCCUUHMIMIAVROAAPSLQMIAB
HMIBODZZWNQYYMUFAWFYHELTTESAHXVKEPW
MOOQDKNATZPHFQITMIATQMIAZFBJQQMIAJV
MSSSTZUXBGPRABRYWFPQKDEPFVWWGATLGNR
HQLQMHDSUMIAQKJZALGMJYNDVPYIDLMDFZN
LCIFMWOPXIHSBNRULVJWGLAFMIAUMCBROKN
AQCICYMIAQVRWVRTQXJSAIFHGNNROEMIAHK
SIMMIAJWMIAUDFIBZNCBOOJBMIAOBYSMIAX
SLAILFVNAUIKAZAVEWGZORGNMMIAMLARLKL
JBGLVDORRJAQQOWOAMIAMIAPIMEWCLUFMIA
SREMIAMIAGXVHJMIAXMIABWDIJXPMIARIYC
JBGYUAADXMKIMIAGDPGVWMIAVNFPKTABNEZ
HETMAWSOIMIAWRZOXIMIAMRMWEMHCPXFOTY
PKGGUAYMIYMQXGAYYQXMIAAKBPMIAFRPCWT
EFCFNJXZCKJQOBCKBXLJHZXCCFAFDTBSUKF
XQKZGTXDDRCCDCPXFAIMIAYVOSZTDCCDWRN
AVSSLEHYQLDYDMIAGJLUOIOETLLMIAWERRD
HBCMIAMINJXRXKAEPRMYFMIAMIANHDMIAWO
```

30	4
6	12
40	20
57	24
55	27
63	25
8	25
12	28
17	26
22	30
12	42
35	26
25	6
19	30
8	16
4	20
8	1
24	45
12	24
2	25

Are you sure? See page 194!

CALCULATE

2 • 3 = _____		13 - 4 = _____
10 + 6 = _____		7 • 5 = _____
2 • 8 = _____		13 - 13 = _____
2 • 7 = _____		3 • 5 = _____
10 - 5 = _____		8 + 7 = _____
19 - 10 = _____		5 • 4 = _____
8 + 4 = _____		10 + 9 = _____
6 - 4 = _____		7 • 2 = _____
4 + 8 = _____		3 • 7 = _____
2 + 18 = _____		8 + 16 = _____
2 + 12 = _____		4 • 10 = _____
18 - 8 = _____		5 + 12 = _____
2 • 9 = _____		17 + 8 = _____
5 + 11 = _____		28 - 28 = _____
20 - 2 = _____		23 - 17 = _____
19 - 11 = _____		26 - 23 = _____
4 • 5 = _____		5 • 8 = _____
5 • 3 = _____		6 • 5 = _____
8 - 7 = _____		15 + 14 = _____
12 + 5 = _____		20 + 8 = _____

Additional tasks - only for math lovers!

$20 + 10 =$ _____ $2 \cdot 2 =$ _____

$39 - 33 =$ _____ $6 \cdot 2 =$ _____

$45 - 5 =$ _____ $11 + 9 =$ _____

$28 + 29 =$ _____ $17 + 7 =$ _____

$31 + 24 =$ _____ $15 + 12 =$ _____

$9 \cdot 7 =$ _____ $7 + 18 =$ _____

$4 \cdot 2 =$ _____ $16 + 9 =$ _____

$2 \cdot 6 =$ _____ $7 \cdot 4 =$ _____

$34 - 17 =$ _____ $22 + 4 =$ _____

$14 + 8 =$ _____ $10 \cdot 3 =$ _____

$4 \cdot 3 =$ _____ $6 \cdot 7 =$ _____

$5 \cdot 7 =$ _____ $10 + 16 =$ _____

$31 - 6 =$ _____ $27 - 21 =$ _____

$50 - 31 =$ _____ $7 + 23 =$ _____

$2 \cdot 4 =$ _____ $2 \cdot 8 =$ _____

$14 - 10 =$ _____ $12 + 8 =$ _____

$47 - 39 =$ _____ $20 - 19 =$ _____

$3 \cdot 8 =$ _____ $9 \cdot 5 =$ _____

$3 \cdot 4 =$ _____ $6 \cdot 4 =$ _____

$31 - 29 =$ _____ $20 + 5 =$ _____

FIND THE NUMBERS!

6	9
16	35
16	0
14	15
5	15
9	20
12	19
2	14
12	21
20	24
14	40
10	17
18	25
16	0
18	6
8	3
20	40
15	30
1	29
17	28

Mark and count: 1

```
6 2 9 8 9 3 6 9 5 2 7 4 2 9 0 1 4 0
1 1 3 7 2 6 6 5 9 2 3 9 0 5 8 9 3 7
0 3 9 1 0 4 3 7 1 2 4 0 4 4 2 9 9 8
6 1 5 7 8 7 4 2 1 3 5 6 2 7 4 6 4 4
8 7 7 7 8 8 1 3 3 2 4 0 3 3 4 9 6 6
2 7 4 1 0 7 4 7 6 3 6 7 9 3 7 4 9 2
4 5 0 9 7 8 8 9 9 3 9 8 9 0 4 1 1 4
4 9 6 1 1 6 2 3 8 6 3 7 5 9 7 2 6 6
2 3 5 4 0 0 8 5 7 5 0 5 1 7 7 6 1 5
1 2 0 3 3 1 2 3 7 8 3 1 0 0 2 1 9 3
0 6 8 7 9 3 4 0 9 3 8 6 9 3 0 1 7 6
2 9 2 3 6 0 8 4 2 2 7 0 1 2 8 3 3 0
4 9 1 7 6 3 7 7 6 1 5 7 7 6 9 4 5 1
```

Mark and count: 32

```
11 27 93 18 39 36 32 50 98 66 97 38
57 38 64 35 28 27 32 75 86 36 20 61
88 38 93 32 73 73 48 32 72 75 28 92
38 88 32 80 20 36 32 48 61 53 11 54
41 89 35 43 84 65 56 71 34 32 56 23
24 63 73 39 65 93 24 55 24 19 32 62
99 44 80 53 97 22 90 14 99 37 95 85
29 75 32 27 46 97 43 98 74 49 88 80
15 32 93 45 27 32 39 21 36 52 63 79
14 34 44 38 77 13 59 54 16 12 52 43
32 26 95 47 89 93 86 32 36 47 59 67
91 32 58 32 77 43 64 32 32 13 96 38
55 46 79 89 17 61 90 79 51 83 22 90
```

Are you sure? See page 195!

Now make a simple sketch of the memorized picture with as many details as possible:

TRY TO REMEMBER!

What should you find?

- City: _____
- Name: _____
- Decrypted text: _____

day 12

WARM UP!

7 − 3 = _____	12 + 10 = _____
15 − 14 = _____	13 + 10 = _____
6 + 5 = _____	9 − 5 = _____
2 • 7 = _____	29 − 5 = _____
10 • 2 = _____	26 − 19 = _____
16 − 5 = _____	19 + 5 = _____
4 • 6 = _____	21 + 6 = _____
4 + 10 = _____	4 • 4 = _____
20 − 4 = _____	4 + 20 = _____
14 − 3 = _____	7 • 5 = _____
6 + 4 = _____	13 + 12 = _____
11 + 5 = _____	3 • 10 = _____
7 + 11 = _____	21 − 10 = _____
6 • 3 = _____	8 • 5 = _____
2 • 3 = _____	20 − 11 = _____
16 − 2 = _____	2 • 5 = _____
18 − 14 = _____	17 + 10 = _____
3 • 7 = _____	28 − 5 = _____
20 − 12 = _____	17 − 4 = _____
5 + 6 = _____	8 + 10 = _____

Decipher the following code with the "Caesar encryption".

The required character offset to the right is: 3

P Q Y Q B X L C

_ _ _ _ _ _ _ _

Copy the decrypted text on page 197.

ABCDEFGHIJKLMNOPQRSTUVWXYZ_ABCDEF

Memorize this picture and all of its details as best as you can to make a sketch of it later.

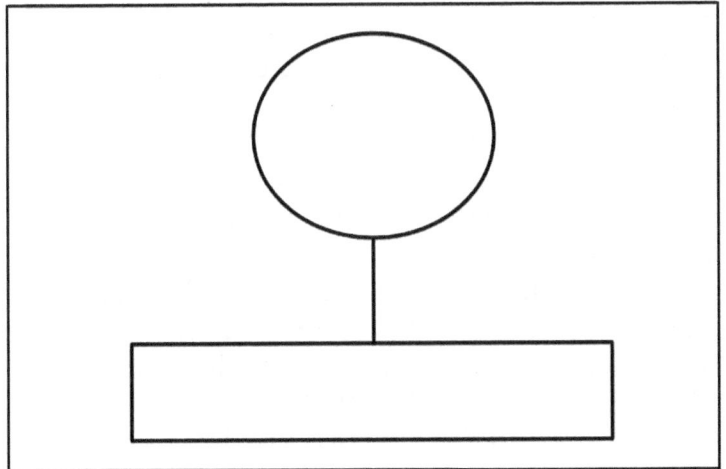

4	22
1	23
11	4
14	24
20	7
11	24
24	27
14	16
16	24
11	35
10	25
16	30
18	11
18	40
6	9
14	10
4	27
21	23
8	13
11	18

Mark and count: I

```
LILLLLLLLLILLLLLLLLLLLLLLLLLLLLLLLLL
LLLLLLLLLLILLLLLLLLLILLLLLLLLLLLLLLL
LLLLLLLLLLLLLLLLLLLLLLLLLLLLLLLLLLLL
LLLLLLLLLLLLLLLILLLLLILLLLLLLLLLLLLL
LLLLLLLILLLLLLLLILLLLLILLLLLLLLLLLLL
LLLLLLILLLLLLLLLIILLLLLLLLLLLLLLLLLL
LLLLLLLLLLLLLLLLLLLLLLLLLLLLLLLLLLLL
LLLLLLLLLLLLLLLLLLLILLLLLLLLLLLLLLLL
LLLLLLLLLLLLLLLLLLILLLLLLLLLLLLLLLLL
LLLLLLILLLLLLLLLLLLILLILLLLLLLLLLLLI
LLLLILLLLLLLLLLLLLLLLLLLLLLLLLLLILLL
LLLLLLLLLILLLLLLLLLLIILLLLLLLILLLLLL
LLILLILLLLLLLLLLLLLLLLLLLLLLLILLLLLL
```

Mark and count: DEHLI

```
ILEEDHLLLLDHELIIIHDEHLIDHLDDIEDDLHL
EIIHDEHLIDDILEHLLLHEEELDEHLIDDIDIEL
EDEEEDIDEHLIHDIDEHDEHLIEIIDEHLIIILI
EDEHLIIEDEHLIDIHHDLLIHLIHEHDDIDEHLI
LDLIIDEHLIDDLIIEEHDEHLIEDEDHIHHILDH
EHIIDEIELHEHHHHDIDDIHDHHHLDHHIHHLEE
ELEHDDDHHDDEHHLEDIDLIEHHEDDEIHLLIHD
IIHDEHLIEIIIDIEIELLLDLEEILLELDLLDIE
EIHELHDEIDDDLIEHIHEIELHIDDIDHHEDLDE
HDEIHELEDELEHIDEDDEDHDEHLIELIILEHLH
DHLHEIDDDLDLHIHIDHDHILIDHDDEHHHHDED
IEDIDEHLIDEHLIHELEHIIELELEILIDIIHLL
IDHDLLILDEHLIHDLHLDDIHDEIHILDLEHELH
```

Decrypted original text from the previous page:
STATE OF

Mark and count: ALICE

```
RALICEBUXBBPURGHTOFTLVATPXTYPALICEG
ICMRNRUBZZKPBHWVKTVXMSWEYNYZBIOFPDU
RVWLHALICERZZIXPSSWMUSHWCPIGHAEOTYN
XDGOAJAREDZIOKQALICEOLUHESMZIKHWNZW
QQTPXBUXDRDCJALICETGLONCEMZIEMALICE
HUEMOOWHSSQIHWALICEUHMCZDCDHQTQBCRP
UATFNUBZHLITSAZIDEFAOALICEDACCLRABG
ALICEGXDRTIUGHALICEVTPWEHIIQAPTNEUK
LVYXWZFAWKSQBHLQQJBMPGTWSLALICELZXX
TSJYCQBBTRALICEQUALICEYLDEVCALICEQK
STLMGQJZOXOUDMEUZXHTVAFNWKDQXTFFPQX
XHISJJCBQSPVMBLKOARYDSCLLDEFYXBLDDY
TKIMZEDYYEPNNCEHKALICEGBUJEFCZKEJLU
DZIGLJUDULNDSSOWYRWAYIDHIGRNGTDDOOC
CJEIYXBICMYLFOSGMTAVWOYBNEDUGJORSHP
CEKCQMSJZWGLIQMBXAHHLUCLFQVHWQEWCAA
EEBLDISJJWOQREMPHYAOOXDNPPBWSFLZRYD
YDAJTPKFLSZSLBFKAALICEGGWALICEFHVHH
DSWVOFPFSPALICEALICESVIHIMQMMYHYKII
CUPQRRALICETOFOWFHCFTGKSRHRALICEPQV
IALICEBARBZJOALICEFALICECXPNUFYIIME
RALICEALICEPHVANSWCXWORXFKPKDIMYTOK
ALICEDOXJXNEALICEZGJVKYBEIMSGDLBUGL
ALICEUVUHQVZCADHEZIKVBYONWNFWFOUVWF
ZUWALICEKTSRBWWVWXKUIRALICEWCXMMQUM
ETGOLADALICENKPMKXPALICETBEALICETHJ
OXDWSBULJPWFOATUBRRUHTALICEIBQZKGID
TIMMUCVAGEVMZWGHBBNSHUWALICEXBLSGMI
RTALICEYMNZVGYEKBCODZALICEOBOSSXMGM
```

90	30
10	2
22	23
35	20
56	30
32	0
70	12
80	20
9	24
48	14
64	23
63	18
1	20
48	24
39	4
13	10
9	11
37	30
47	12
54	9

Are you sure? See page 194!

CALCULATE

4 + 14 = _____	4 • 4 = _____
3 + 13 = _____	5 + 8 = _____
13 - 2 = _____	27 - 11 = _____
2 • 5 = _____	22 + 6 = _____
5 - 3 = _____	5 • 3 = _____
4 • 6 = _____	20 + 9 = _____
10 - 10 = _____	26 - 26 = _____
15 - 10 = _____	11 + 16 = _____
19 - 17 = _____	22 - 11 = _____
11 + 9 = _____	6 • 2 = _____
10 - 2 = _____	3 • 9 = _____
2 • 2 = _____	19 - 3 = _____
8 + 12 = _____	9 • 2 = _____
2 • 9 = _____	5 • 9 = _____
11 + 8 = _____	7 • 6 = _____
7 • 2 = _____	10 + 17 = _____
16 - 3 = _____	21 - 14 = _____
4 + 6 = _____	2 • 4 = _____
10 + 10 = _____	3 • 5 = _____
6 • 3 = _____	16 + 11 = _____

Additional tasks - only for math lovers!

$9 \cdot 10 =$ _____ $3 \cdot 10 =$ _____

$5 \cdot 2 =$ _____ $9 - 7 =$ _____

$8 + 14 =$ _____ $19 + 4 =$ _____

$5 \cdot 7 =$ _____ $14 + 6 =$ _____

$18 + 38 =$ _____ $20 + 10 =$ _____

$26 + 6 =$ _____ $4 - 4 =$ _____

$10 \cdot 7 =$ _____ $2 \cdot 6 =$ _____

$10 \cdot 8 =$ _____ $2 \cdot 10 =$ _____

$42 - 33 =$ _____ $3 \cdot 8 =$ _____

$8 \cdot 6 =$ _____ $25 - 11 =$ _____

$8 \cdot 8 =$ _____ $17 + 6 =$ _____

$9 \cdot 7 =$ _____ $6 \cdot 3 =$ _____

$25 - 24 =$ _____ $5 \cdot 4 =$ _____

$27 + 21 =$ _____ $12 + 12 =$ _____

$15 + 24 =$ _____ $2 \cdot 2 =$ _____

$47 - 34 =$ _____ $26 - 16 =$ _____

$40 - 31 =$ _____ $26 - 15 =$ _____

$46 - 9 =$ _____ $5 \cdot 6 =$ _____

$10 + 37 =$ _____ $4 \cdot 3 =$ _____

$25 + 29 =$ _____ $3 \cdot 3 =$ _____

18	16
16	13
11	16
10	28
2	15
24	29
0	0
5	27
2	11
20	12
8	27
4	16
20	18
18	45
19	42
14	27
13	7
10	8
20	15
18	27

Mark and count: 8

```
7 6 0 3 3 2 8 4 7 7 1 8 2 3 0 4 2 1
8 5 9 2 3 6 9 0 8 8 5 0 9 0 8 0 0 2
2 9 2 8 3 3 5 6 8 0 5 2 0 2 6 1 4 0
6 4 0 8 2 2 1 0 4 1 4 1 6 1 7 2 1 0
9 3 0 2 6 7 4 4 4 9 4 5 4 2 2 2 4 1
6 6 8 6 2 4 2 8 5 2 2 4 5 9 6 7 0 9
7 6 6 5 9 0 1 3 9 6 4 1 8 1 9 9 5 8
7 2 4 9 7 7 1 4 5 9 0 1 1 0 0 4 6 2
1 8 5 7 3 8 5 4 4 6 0 3 6 7 8 0 4 6
5 3 8 8 4 8 1 5 7 8 3 4 2 2 0 6 0 2
1 2 4 2 3 3 8 5 4 0 6 6 0 8 6 7 4 5
4 7 3 4 3 0 1 5 6 0 7 6 0 9 7 5 2 1
2 3 6 7 6 1 5 7 0 6 7 1 8 4 8 7 9 4
```

Mark and count: 64

```
54 86 97 65 79 77 53 71 76 86 42 44
64 23 21 64 74 64 92 64 69 55 67 51
77 61 27 85 50 88 63 10 82 64 64 72
37 38 95 22 16 30 64 64 64 64 64 80
64 48 98 53 45 25 97 30 10 64 94 93
12 96 21 76 64 64 36 70 64 98 40 90
99 64 80 94 68 24 61 91 68 80 71 64
70 54 14 23 47 59 68 31 39 71 87 64
44 37 80 28 61 22 99 51 67 46 72 64
64 50 44 66 65 41 34 32 36 53 13 94
93 36 57 66 78 77 54 77 56 22 92 78
46 42 82 45 58 50 24 80 91 11 64 87
96 81 11 81 64 34 37 38 64 29 64 27
```

Are you sure? See page 195!

Now make a simple sketch of the memorized picture
with as many details as possible:

TRY TO REMEMBER!

What should you find?

- City: _____
- Name: _____
- Decrypted text: _____

day 13

WARM UP!

9 - 6 = _____	6 + 15 = _____
8 + 5 = _____	29 - 8 = _____
10 - 4 = _____	6 + 12 = _____
3 • 2 = _____	11 + 5 = _____
7 • 2 = _____	6 + 24 = _____
8 + 6 = _____	4 + 8 = _____
2 + 10 = _____	18 - 17 = _____
9 + 3 = _____	5 + 19 = _____
6 • 2 = _____	18 - 8 = _____
15 - 2 = _____	5 + 7 = _____
7 + 8 = _____	6 + 21 = _____
7 - 4 = _____	6 • 4 = _____
4 • 4 = _____	24 - 3 = _____
8 + 9 = _____	26 + 4 = _____
10 + 10 = _____	7 • 6 = _____
3 + 11 = _____	11 - 3 = _____
4 • 6 = _____	13 + 5 = _____
2 + 2 = _____	9 + 5 = _____
2 + 6 = _____	3 • 5 = _____
3 • 7 = _____	18 + 4 = _____

Decipher the following code with the
"Caesar encryption".

The required character offset to the
right is: 5

O C _ V W M O

_ _ _ _ _ _ _

Copy the decrypted text on page 197.

ABCDEFGHIJKLMNOPQRSTUVWXYZ_ABCDEF

Memorize this picture and all of its
details as best as you can to make a
sketch of it later.

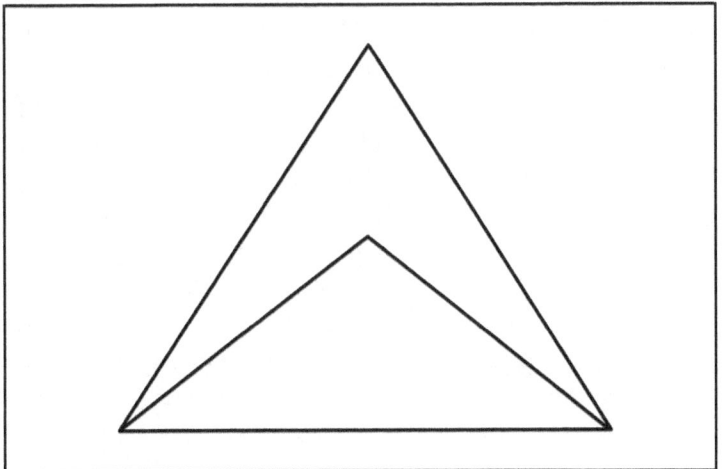

WORDS AND LETTERS

3	21
13	21
6	18
6	16
14	30
14	12
12	1
12	24
12	10
13	12
15	27
3	24
16	21
17	30
20	42
14	8
24	18
4	14
8	15
21	22

Mark and count: O

```
CCCCCCCCCCCCCCCCCCCCCOCCCCCCCCCCCCCCCCC
CCCCCCCOCCCCCCCCCCCCCCOCCCCCCCCCCCCCCC
CCCCCCCCCCCCCCCCCCCCCCCCCCCCCCCCCCCCC
CCCCCCCCCCCCCCCCCCOCCCCCCCCCCCCCCCCCC
CCCCCCCCCCCCCCCCCCCCCCCCCCOCCCCCCCCCC
CCCCCCCCCCCCCCCCCCCCCOCCCCOCCCCCCCCC
CCCCCCCCCCCCCCOCCCCCCCCCCCCCOCCOCCCC
CCOCOCCCCCCCCCCCCCCCCCCCCCCCCCCCCCC
CCCCCCCCCCCCCCOCCCCCCCCCCCCCOCCCCOC
CCCCCCCCCCCCCCCCCCCCCCCCCCCCCCCCCCC
CCCCCCCCCCCCCCCCCCCCCCCCCCCCCCCCCCC
CCCCCCCCCCCCCCCCCCCCOOCCCCCCCCCCCC
CCCCCCCCCCCCCCCCCCCCCOCCCCCCCCCCCC
```

Mark and count: BOGOTA

```
BOAOAOGOAOGTOTOABOGOTABOGOTAGBOGOTA
BOGOTABOGOTABGTBGBABGBAOGBTOGTTTATG
OOBOBAABTOTBBOGOTAOBGBOGOTATOATTAOO
TTAATAOOOOAATBAOATOBGOBBOGOTAABGOGT
OOBOGOTAAGBOGOTAATBOGOTABOGOTAGTOOT
BBOGOTAOOAOBOAOOATBOGOTAOAABTOTTOOO
TBOTOTOGBGTTOBTBOGBOGOTAABAOAGBGGGO
OBOGABOGOTAOBOGTABOAOGTAAGTOAOGGATT
TOBGTAOOOTBBAGBOOGTTBBGBOGOTAOOOBBB
TGAGAOOBOOGBBBBOTAOAGGGBGAAATGATAAG
GBOGAGAGTOOBAOATBOOOATOGAOOOBOATGAB
ABTBBTTTGTTTTAGGTOTABOGOTAOBAOAAOTT
OOTAGAGGBOATBGOTOTOBBTGOOAOAAABOAAA
```

Decrypted original text from the previous page:
THE ART

Mark and count: OSCAR

KGMZLJWRGVYMVYJCHNSPTWXZOSCARWABVKO
OSCARZAYHHOEYFGGRZWUXFSWUDTHAIQKDFD
BUICZPMDMWTZTZPPRCOFQLVOCCJUZDGLPEH
OOUJDMNZOCNTLMRIXOSCARXPZVUUWVLZWWY
ZOARKMBOZRNFFLOSCARCOSCARHZQOOYRDCH
ZFDSXGVMWUSMIOKOZVMFGFZHPZOSCARMXQK
PWUSVKPNRVOSCARZDOWGCONEPPOSCARDRVE
YPEMWGZLHPLMKOSCARSMOSCARIUUPDXTNJF
BFXOSCARKNMJCRRJIJNRFFAIAKVTNOHCPOV
NAJAGEFOSCARWBYMVTGUJOSCAROSCARIJED
LNKCBOAULECOSCARWHCLBZLJSOSCARKQLBR
CVWCCZOSCARWWYNKCXOSCARLOSCARIXABGG
NAOSCARSVMRWHOSCAROSCARMIULXIONJPBE
OESWNHHGUWDKCDKLKHGQKVDTMFHOSCARBKQ
ZLRGVXABOSCARQWHPWVHKHNCOOSCARROVJP
WRDZTLWMYANRNUMNXNSVFIFZEAAESMJRRQA
OSCARAOSCARHVGDSUAHCFPRBQZPFFYIQOYV
LPBHZGTRMOSCAROSCARSUWUJOFOSCARTZXT
OSCARVSOKOPPRYQQSCOMVRXMGQAUWGKELIG
CVGTEKLVYRDKLQIFEYRGBCWBHKRKUUEUEXZ
YOSCARQXVPMPNOKTJOJXPOWOSCARWRUGKNK
ZSEEFLOSCAROSCARNIJYDNPMHJPXKHKBNWN
RGFUNTGGEOSCARAZFLOSCARSOSCARZTCFPL
SGJTWHOSCAROSCARVSFCNNQOSCARNUQTFCW
SOTUGXRWXDTVSNVLSRJCMZEOSCAROSCARKZ
DKTXZOSCARJAOSCARIWBSRMDMAPANAETRTA
DBMQITNZULULFYCFFSZRJZOSCARJVOOSCAR
NOSCAROGTIMBIVHMBDIBCZZIHZDLKOKBZQE
LUXNUEGCAGVOBKXVHQOSCARZCUHHIIOJSMB

59	14
37	14
20	24
24	20
32	13
30	25
70	27
42	28
36	24
37	36
47	16
54	27
0	16
54	8
10	24
27	28
9	13
54	21
54	20
15	26

Are you sure? See page 194!

CALCULATE

14 - 6 = _____	8 • 3 = _____
4 • 2 = _____	4 + 14 = _____
7 + 8 = _____	28 - 7 = _____
13 - 3 = _____	6 + 17 = _____
8 + 3 = _____	6 • 8 = _____
2 + 7 = _____	7 • 3 = _____
2 + 4 = _____	10 • 2 = _____
7 + 10 = _____	5 • 6 = _____
4 • 4 = _____	18 + 10 = _____
15 - 9 = _____	24 - 9 = _____
16 - 8 = _____	5 + 8 = _____
20 - 17 = _____	2 • 4 = _____
3 - 3 = _____	5 • 4 = _____
18 - 5 = _____	30 - 12 = _____
19 - 8 = _____	26 + 4 = _____
20 - 18 = _____	4 + 19 = _____
9 - 9 = _____	3 • 2 = _____
4 • 6 = _____	21 + 6 = _____
2 + 11 = _____	9 • 4 = _____
3 + 12 = _____	13 + 8 = _____

34 + 25 = ____   4 + 10 = ____

31 + 6 = ____   29 - 15 = ____

29 - 9 = ____   4 • 6 = ____

44 - 20 = ____   4 • 5 = ____

8 • 4 = ____   19 - 6 = ____

19 + 11 = ____   17 + 8 = ____

10 • 7 = ____   9 • 3 = ____

47 - 5 = ____   23 + 5 = ____

20 + 16 = ____   6 + 18 = ____

25 + 12 = ____   6 • 6 = ____

33 + 14 = ____   8 • 2 = ____

6 • 9 = ____   16 + 11 = ____

31 - 31 = ____   10 + 6 = ____

22 + 32 = ____   18 - 10 = ____

2 • 5 = ____   19 + 5 = ____

44 - 17 = ____   7 • 4 = ____

3 • 3 = ____   17 - 4 = ____

26 + 28 = ____   6 + 15 = ____

38 + 16 = ____   14 + 6 = ____

3 • 5 = ____   15 + 11 = ____

FIND THE NUMBERS!

8	24
8	18
15	21
10	23
11	48
9	21
6	20
17	30
16	28
6	15
8	13
3	8
0	20
13	18
11	30
2	23
0	6
24	27
13	36
15	21

Mark and count: 3

```
6 3 5 3 0 0 8 1 4 9 2 8 5 2 1 0 9 4
7 9 7 8 4 1 8 7 9 3 9 9 0 0 0 4 2 1
0 0 0 0 7 0 7 4 4 2 3 6 7 6 0 0 4 2
6 9 7 3 6 1 5 5 5 8 7 1 5 7 8 7 1 5
4 6 8 3 5 0 3 5 3 1 9 5 2 0 2 4 9 1
6 7 1 6 2 1 6 2 8 4 1 3 5 2 9 5 9 2
6 7 1 9 0 3 2 2 9 6 9 6 0 1 3 0 5 0
1 2 5 0 1 2 4 9 1 2 8 6 6 5 7 0 5 9
3 3 7 8 8 4 1 4 1 8 3 0 3 9 7 0 2 7
5 4 1 6 7 4 8 8 1 2 5 8 7 6 0 8 2 9
9 5 9 7 8 8 1 2 7 9 4 9 3 7 9 5 3 4
8 2 1 0 8 5 1 2 6 5 1 2 7 9 9 8 9 7
1 4 3 1 0 9 2 6 3 9 8 8 0 0 5 8 7 3
```

Mark and count: 78

```
90 54 23 98 58 78 60 65 88 58 64 73
83 14 78 25 56 84 95 30 78 77 14 96
71 40 29 69 43 78 48 60 39 44 15 11
26 65 81 78 90 27 17 37 76 50 16 65
78 81 73 69 35 45 64 59 45 41 78 78
67 78 91 97 34 21 76 29 14 78 78 68
41 95 15 21 48 85 54 96 92 53 34 82
80 78 77 81 33 29 78 34 57 42 78 97
57 66 94 60 98 78 66 38 96 90 87 40
31 96 46 95 83 53 36 46 80 93 73 92
88 37 95 84 96 84 55 78 78 53 89 10
78 36 78 46 78 78 99 78 92 71 15 78
18 76 86 48 43 57 16 56 30 78 11 78
```

Are you sure? See page 195!

Now make a simple sketch of the memorized picture
with as many details as possible:

```



```

TRY TO REMEMBER!

What should you find?

- City: _____
- Name: _____
- Decrypted text: _____

day 14

WARM UP!

12 + 4 = _____	17 - 6 = _____
13 + 7 = _____	9 + 8 = _____
3 • 6 = _____	18 + 5 = _____
20 - 4 = _____	9 • 5 = _____
3 • 4 = _____	18 + 8 = _____
2 + 18 = _____	3 • 9 = _____
3 • 8 = _____	19 - 13 = _____
10 + 8 = _____	27 - 15 = _____
15 - 7 = _____	11 + 19 = _____
5 • 2 = _____	14 - 10 = _____
2 • 3 = _____	4 • 4 = _____
18 - 14 = _____	5 + 23 = _____
3 • 2 = _____	4 + 15 = _____
3 • 7 = _____	2 • 5 = _____
9 - 3 = _____	10 • 2 = _____
8 - 5 = _____	21 + 8 = _____
2 • 2 = _____	7 • 3 = _____
8 + 9 = _____	13 - 10 = _____
20 - 18 = _____	26 - 15 = _____
10 + 3 = _____	6 • 2 = _____

day 14

Decipher the following code with the
"Caesar encryption".

The required character offset to the
right is: 2

U C J J Y B M L C

_ _ _ _ _ _ _ _ _

Copy the decrypted text on page 197.

ABCDEFGHIJKLMNOPQRSTUVWXYZ_ABCDEF

Memorize this picture and all of its
details as best as you can to make a
sketch of it later.

WORDS AND LETTERS

16 11

20 17

18 23

16 45

12 26

20 27

24 6

18 12

8 30

10 4

6 16

4 28

6 19

21 10

6 20

3 29

4 21

17 3

2 11

13 12

Mark and count: P

BBBBBBBBPBPBBBBBBBBBBBBBBBBBBBBBBBBBBB
BBBBBBBBBBBBBBBBBBBBBBBBBBBBBPBBBPBB
BBBBBBBBBBBBBPBBBBBBBBBBBBBBPBBBBBBBB
BBBBBBBBBBBBBBBBBBBBBBBBBBBPBBBBBBBBB
BBBBBBBBBBBBBBBBBBBBBBBBBBBPBBBBBBBBB
BBBBBBBBBBBBBBPBPBBBBBBBBBBBBBBBBBBBB
BBBBBBBBPBBBBBBBPBBBBBBBBBBBBBBBBBBB
BBBBBBBBBBBBBBBBBBBBBBBPBBBBBBBBBBBP
BBBBBBBBBBBBBBBBBBBBBBBBBBBBBBBBBBBBB
BBBBBBBBBBBBBBBBBBBBBBBBBBBBBBBPBBB
BBBBBBBBBBBBBBBBBBBBBBBBBBPBBBBPBBBB
BBBBBBBBBBBBBBBBPBBBBBBBBBBPBBBBBBBB
BBBBBBBBBPBBBBBBBBBBBBBBBBBBBBPBBPB

Mark and count: OTTAWA

TWWTTTOWOAWTATTAAOAOWTATAOTTAWAATOO
WTATTTAWAWWAWATTOAOOOTOTAATWWATTTTA
TWOTTAWATAAWOOOOOATATTWOTTAWAOTOTTO
OWWTTTTWATTWTAOTTAWAAAAWTTATAWATWOW
OTTAWAOOAOOTWWTWAWTATOTTWAAOTTAWATW
WTAATTTWOOAAOWWOAAOTTAWATWTAOATOTAW
TTTATAATATTTOTTAWAWAAWTATOTTAWAAATO
AOATTAWTTATAAOTTAWAAOATATTTOTTAWAO
TTOTTAWAAWTAATOOTTAWATTAATTOAOAWATA
OTOTAWTOAAOTAAAWWATAWWAAATTOTOTTAWA
AOTTAWAOWOTTAWAAWTTTAOWTAOAAOWWAOWA
OATAWOTWWTTTAOAOAOTTAWAWAWATAOOTAOW
TTAATOATOOOTTAWAOTOAWAATATATAAWWTTA

Decrypted original text from the previous page:
WELL DONE

Mark and count: GRACE

```
VMGRACEGRACELCWHZFRXAEGRACEHSOQELSC
CRTKVFQAMIPRNTRULNKNHKASCGSGTVCKWTM
MMJNPSOOZAQKZDVVUWGACGGGRACESLRWQAS
GBMCVMVWLAFKGRACEJGZPIJRMIYQPZZPMIG
WKTZBEWNGRACEAGXNFDCAGRACEVCVHGRACE
TKYTNPNDVMLVKBKGNCGRACEASPOHTNREAET
SMXMATZLKGRACEJVYLTTGGRACEVDETAMYCD
GRACEZGRACEJUCGRACEVGRACEUNQPTPCUXO
JRZMZONBPRGRACEFGRACEQOSMIDWFQCLLNX
MNEZCZUVDTAMXBXWPJOGGRACEYDNJCLJQCW
OPYHGRACEOBHYGBIMQAFGRACEIQGISTEPIK
YNETEWGRACEQVVGPSVDWAMOVZPBEZPDGAEY
GRACEDDVGCAOQBPYNGTVEOQJSRTECRAACYD
KLCWOVQTCGRACEBXINNGRACEFAHXGRACEWM
GRACEMLULESEFHOXVDGPRGXEUMUCGCRNSWI
EETZWYBGRACEUEBPGDCBKVZYDRUJDFEICZT
GRACEAEGVDLGRACEZZDIKPYGRACEKGRACEW
PGRACECNNEHQJIPJLSGRACEAPZWJGRACEYP
SJCCFCGUTOWMZZCBWKJPMPGPVSRBGRWACUB
CKKFOSWTSYWYYTMDSMLGRACEXGSASFEZGAU
ELFCBMRAGRACENVTJSAGRACEIMOFMPXWSMJ
SHFSFHTGRACEYRXAAQDWYMSJNWEOQPFMRUU
NVIBNPVPVCYMAYXHFTXVXOSPYGRACEQKQMZ
XSQSNJDTGTSTFYNUKVRDTTLMVUVZGRACEQX
OJMLQTBGSBENXXRUDYKKXCMSGAFBYMEFIGB
MRYJPIXZCBJDTPTEZNBCMZXTLKGRACENTMB
CMVBAODLIZCGYGRACEEMGRACEUTPRCOBRDU
MBINVGRACEDFLKSMZHDTRTBAEPJBHVOYMIZ
QZUFPAAWXHFJCLGRACEVLAXOEMNJONDISGK
```

42	5
7	6
42	28
24	11
13	29
24	6
9	0
8	40
29	25
26	4
9	28
51	25
43	14
14	49
6	3
1	10
90	13
14	42
50	40
47	21

Are you sure? See page 194!

CALCULATE

14 - 3 = _____	12 + 14 = _____
9 - 5 = _____	13 + 7 = _____
11 - 4 = _____	2 • 9 = _____
3 • 4 = _____	3 • 6 = _____
7 • 3 = _____	13 + 12 = _____
14 - 11 = _____	8 • 4 = _____
10 + 5 = _____	4 • 5 = _____
2 • 3 = _____	26 - 20 = _____
13 - 3 = _____	21 - 21 = _____
12 + 2 = _____	30 - 27 = _____
18 - 16 = _____	2 • 5 = _____
16 - 2 = _____	10 - 8 = _____
17 + 3 = _____	5 + 24 = _____
7 - 3 = _____	14 + 12 = _____
5 • 2 = _____	24 - 10 = _____
4 • 4 = _____	27 - 23 = _____
8 • 3 = _____	7 • 4 = _____
17 - 3 = _____	21 + 4 = _____
7 + 11 = _____	5 • 9 = _____
3 • 5 = _____	19 + 9 = _____

Additional tasks - only for math lovers!

11 + 31 = _____	30 - 25 = _____
14 - 7 = _____	2 • 3 = _____
32 + 10 = _____	4 • 7 = _____
43 - 19 = _____	5 + 6 = _____
45 - 32 = _____	19 + 10 = _____
9 + 15 = _____	16 - 10 = _____
3 • 3 = _____	27 - 27 = _____
39 - 31 = _____	5 • 8 = _____
12 + 17 = _____	18 + 7 = _____
41 - 15 = _____	10 - 6 = _____
28 - 19 = _____	12 + 16 = _____
13 + 38 = _____	12 + 13 = _____
29 + 14 = _____	7 • 2 = _____
7 + 7 = _____	7 • 7 = _____
3 • 2 = _____	12 - 9 = _____
32 - 31 = _____	4 + 6 = _____
10 • 9 = _____	8 + 5 = _____
37 - 23 = _____	7 • 6 = _____
15 + 35 = _____	8 • 5 = _____
11 + 36 = _____	12 + 9 = _____

FIND THE NUMBERS!

<table>
<tr><td>11</td><td>26</td></tr>
<tr><td>4</td><td>20</td></tr>
<tr><td>7</td><td>18</td></tr>
<tr><td>12</td><td>18</td></tr>
<tr><td>21</td><td>25</td></tr>
<tr><td>3</td><td>32</td></tr>
<tr><td>15</td><td>20</td></tr>
<tr><td>6</td><td>6</td></tr>
<tr><td>10</td><td>0</td></tr>
<tr><td>14</td><td>3</td></tr>
<tr><td>2</td><td>10</td></tr>
<tr><td>14</td><td>2</td></tr>
<tr><td>20</td><td>29</td></tr>
<tr><td>4</td><td>26</td></tr>
<tr><td>10</td><td>14</td></tr>
<tr><td>16</td><td>4</td></tr>
<tr><td>24</td><td>28</td></tr>
<tr><td>14</td><td>25</td></tr>
<tr><td>18</td><td>45</td></tr>
<tr><td>15</td><td>28</td></tr>
</table>

Mark and count: 5

```
7 2 4 7 8 9 9 4 6 4 1 6 2 9 0 9 4 6
5 4 5 8 3 4 4 3 0 9 4 4 4 3 3 1 3 2
3 3 8 7 3 4 8 5 7 3 6 7 1 0 7 9 4 6
8 7 2 2 5 4 4 9 4 6 6 4 8 5 5 0 9 7
7 8 3 3 7 5 1 8 6 8 7 6 1 3 4 2 5 1
2 7 1 9 4 7 8 3 9 5 3 3 2 6 4 9 7 7
5 0 4 9 1 4 7 3 9 4 8 3 0 0 3 5 3 9
9 0 5 7 4 0 5 0 6 8 8 1 8 6 1 7 0 6
3 7 8 8 2 6 3 6 3 8 7 3 0 0 0 4 6 4
7 0 4 7 3 5 5 9 4 7 6 6 7 0 4 3 5 1
4 6 7 6 8 1 1 5 4 7 0 8 7 6 5 2 2 0
0 7 5 4 8 2 8 9 4 2 1 0 9 5 5 2 4 8
6 8 3 6 8 8 4 5 6 8 2 8 5 8 0 1 9 3
```

Mark and count: 47

```
71 29 25 25 52 48 46 27 54 62 67 47
63 48 51 67 80 47 83 31 45 20 30 12
17 42 47 16 47 47 48 47 78 53 39 20
47 36 93 45 47 21 63 54 84 33 62 71
12 71 50 47 88 52 20 36 97 55 96 47
28 26 41 25 53 35 55 27 17 75 85 13
99 25 94 48 25 37 24 12 81 36 92 22
44 58 93 47 89 53 22 63 11 89 60 68
21 51 45 42 28 14 41 98 17 89 39 85
63 30 19 68 14 58 14 47 42 81 72 97
88 69 91 41 47 94 70 65 78 39 21 38
72 88 90 96 90 39 54 68 96 17 47 92
47 61 34 68 63 47 57 98 59 90 63 38
```

Are you sure? See page 195!

Now make a simple sketch of the memorized picture
with as many details as possible:

TRY TO REMEMBER!

What should you find?

- City: _____
- Name: _____
- Decrypted text: _____

day 15

WARM UP!

17 - 5 = _____	9 • 5 = _____
12 - 3 = _____	2 • 4 = _____
2 • 10 = _____	5 + 9 = _____
6 • 4 = _____	12 + 4 = _____
8 - 6 = _____	16 + 8 = _____
8 + 9 = _____	4 • 10 = _____
4 • 2 = _____	29 - 21 = _____
12 - 7 = _____	23 - 19 = _____
13 - 13 = _____	5 • 7 = _____
6 • 2 = _____	4 + 13 = _____
14 + 2 = _____	16 - 7 = _____
14 - 2 = _____	29 - 3 = _____
14 - 5 = _____	4 • 9 = _____
11 + 7 = _____	8 • 3 = _____
3 • 4 = _____	5 • 6 = _____
8 - 2 = _____	22 + 5 = _____
8 • 2 = _____	13 - 6 = _____
7 • 3 = _____	10 - 10 = _____
19 - 16 = _____	12 + 14 = _____
4 • 6 = _____	6 • 5 = _____

Decipher the following code with the "Caesar encryption".

The required character offset to the right is: 4

U K Q W B E J E O D A _

_ _ _ _ _ _ _ _ _ _ _ _

Copy the decrypted text on page 197.

ABCDEFGHIJKLMNOPQRSTUVWXYZ_ABCDEF

Memorize this picture and all of its details as best as you can to make a sketch of it later.

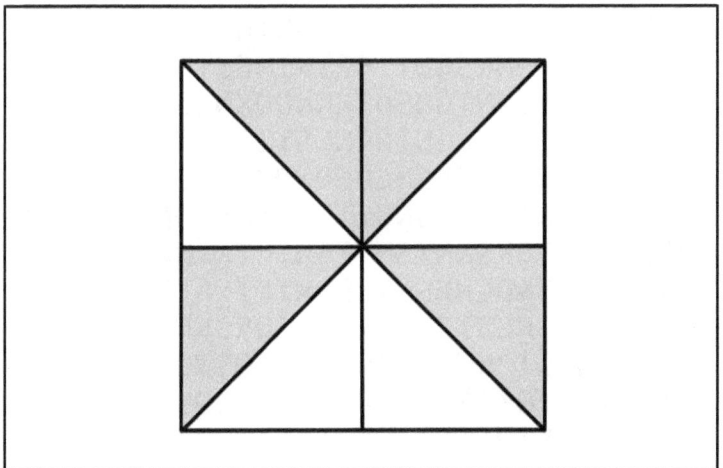

12	45
9	8
20	14
24	16
2	24
17	40
8	8
5	4
0	35
12	17
16	9
12	26
9	36
18	24
12	30
6	27
16	7
21	0
3	26
24	30

Mark and count: S

```
GGGGSGGGGGGGGGGGGGGGGGGSGGGGGGGGGGGGGGGG
GGGGGGGGGGSGGGGGGGGGGGGGGGGGGGGSSGGGGGGG
GGGGGGGGGGGGGGGGSGGGSSGGGGGGGGGGGGGGGGGS
SGGGGGGGGGGGGGGGGGGGGGGGGGGGGGGGGGGGGGSG
GGGGGGGGGGGGGGGGGGGGGSGGGSGGGGGGGGGGGGGG
GGGGGGGGGGGSGGGGGGSGGGGGGGGGGGGSGGGGG
GGGGGGGGGGGGGGGGGGGGGGGGGGGGGGGGGGGGGG
GGGGGGSGGGGGGGGGGGGGGGGGGGGGGGGGGGGGGGG
GGGGGGGGGGGGGGGGGGGGGGGGGGGGGGGSGGGGG
GGGGGGGGGGGGGGGGGGGGGGGGGGGGGGGGGGGGGG
GGGGGGGGGGGGGGGGGGGGGGGGGGGGGGGGGGGGGG
GGGGGGGGGSGGGGGGGSSGGGGGGGGGGGGGGGGGGGG
GGGGGGGGGGGGGGGGGGGGGSGGGGGGGGGGGGGGGG
```

Mark and count: KINGSTON

```
IGKKKKINGSTONKINGSTONOGGKKGKGKSNKSN
SKISINOOSGIKGNIGOKINGSTONNSKNNGNONK
NKINGSTONGNNSGSTTSGTKINGSTONOOSIIKG
KINGSTONTGNNTGNSNSKNNOOKNOSTNTGSSKO
KSISTGGGGNNKNGNINTNNSTITSGTIGTKKNTG
IKINGSTONNTSGSSNGNGNNOKKINGSTONTNNT
IINOGGTIKINGSTONGSTNKINGSTONSKIKITN
GNSOONNSOGKSNNIGNTIONINTKINGSTONSKN
IIKINGSTONOGKNSNNNSSKIKINGSTONOOSOG
SOTTGTKSSNGKISTNGTSOKGOSSKNSNGNGTNK
OOSOKINGSTONNONIOGISKINGSTONONTGNNS
ONTNNIKKIOKGSGKSIKOSINNNOOSTNOGTKST
SNTOKINGSTONISSISKKINGSTONNTINNGNNK
```

158

```
Decrypted original text from the previous page:
YOU FINISHED
```

Mark and count: DANIEL

16	3
3	10
18	5
18	16
45	25
32	1
42	18
80	0
36	24
26	24
42	19
12	2
56	20
33	40
22	30
32	28
2	24
13	12
28	15
56	27

```
VSSMPGSRLUPBAYDWNCDANIELELBVPZICPMU
DANIELQAEIEAMPDANIELUMWGFOTEBNHJTBV
BOOUVEPDANIELKAGAFRPDANIELUJKVVOIMT
DANIELEKWYKDANIELFXUOFBURSNVDDANIEL
DHGCTTZJROSPLYTBUMJTFCMRIJKXSLZPKWX
TECFECIUZGCUAQXIEDANIELTDJZADANIELY
DANIELLUKYUEGDANIELAEWOKGQDPUFABJHJ
UZGNXKJRMADANIELTSDANIELJWTCMMWLVCE
DANIELZISQLJKCGBEIGQZQPXBAULJVQHAZW
KKJITHKPNZDZAQGQZQXCGKZBSSSYGXRHMTN
MDDANIELEVWGADDANIELRRDANIELSEPLSRY
WJDWXLDANIELBCDANIELSWEFDANIELRHUYH
XSWWUBDANIELQHUOPJVDANIELIOFYFPVHCE
SQZQLIQPYXUSOAQCBIKNYEDANIELKQREZVF
ZATODANIELQDANIELEHJLDANIELBDANIELV
PUDANIELDANIELCFYXDANIELUHHKIGLUHJF
IFTXCSHIJDANIELDJETODANIELVNGONNFPG
DANIELYUSDVJJNXNHRIDANIELIIQENLUOJL
AJDDANIELCDANIELXDANIELCFJSSXTWXOSL
OYWJQQXSDANIELWZWLJFPVKDWUGXLKHFORS
TGUEUVUODANIELZEDANIELPCUXIXDOMWHJA
MDANIELSZWHGTRTKSHDDANIELYTNHXGHYTR
OFHWPSCFTFMOCEZYRVGDANIELEOEMVQCKND
RMABVKIHDANIELUVTOSMTXLALBVQIMKXAXS
NCHODANIELBWDANIELAGPAZAMGPXBKSROHB
XPRDNDANIELVEDANIELZFMPFHEKNAINHJLE
ROPDANIELFBXEXESQHVWAWMJNVPARXMRPMM
CACHDANIELIQVOPDANIELDANIELTFIYIPUD
VUNULQRRUBPUXADANIELRXOXECFWVBJPGGM
```

Are you sure? See page 194!

CALCULATE

2 • 9 = _____	15 - 7 = _____
9 + 11 = _____	10 + 6 = _____
8 • 3 = _____	4 • 3 = _____
16 + 2 = _____	22 - 17 = _____
13 - 4 = _____	13 - 10 = _____
9 - 4 = _____	19 + 9 = _____
6 • 4 = _____	24 - 10 = _____
5 + 7 = _____	30 - 27 = _____
7 + 13 = _____	17 - 5 = _____
2 • 3 = _____	9 + 8 = _____
2 + 8 = _____	30 - 14 = _____
2 • 4 = _____	27 - 27 = _____
4 + 15 = _____	5 • 9 = _____
11 + 2 = _____	25 - 6 = _____
2 • 10 = _____	8 + 9 = _____
3 • 8 = _____	24 - 18 = _____
5 • 4 = _____	4 • 9 = _____
9 • 2 = _____	8 - 8 = _____
17 - 11 = _____	20 + 9 = _____
6 • 3 = _____	3 • 7 = _____

day 15

Additional tasks - only for math lovers!

24 - 8 = _____   27 - 24 = _____
24 - 21 = _____   14 - 4 = _____
30 - 12 = _____   30 - 25 = _____
3 • 6 = _____   8 • 2 = _____
12 + 33 = _____   5 • 5 = _____
21 + 11 = _____   10 - 9 = _____
7 • 6 = _____   25 - 7 = _____
8 • 10 = _____   3 - 3 = _____
10 + 26 = _____   27 - 3 = _____
9 + 17 = _____   29 - 5 = _____
10 + 32 = _____   10 + 9 = _____
33 - 21 = _____   6 - 4 = _____
7 • 8 = _____   16 + 4 = _____
38 - 5 = _____   4 • 10 = _____
43 - 21 = _____   5 • 6 = _____
8 • 4 = _____   10 + 18 = _____
43 - 41 = _____   15 + 9 = _____
32 - 19 = _____   6 • 2 = _____
7 • 4 = _____   11 + 4 = _____
32 + 24 = _____   17 + 10 = _____

FIND THE NUMBERS!

18	8
20	16
24	12
18	5
9	3
5	28
24	14
12	3
20	12
6	17
10	16
8	0
19	45
13	19
20	17
24	6
20	36
18	0
6	29
18	21

Mark and count: 7

```
6 9 5 3 2 6 3 7 2 5 8 6 7 0 0 4 1 7
9 3 0 1 3 6 1 9 9 3 3 0 5 7 9 2 8 4
7 1 1 0 9 2 9 5 9 0 2 8 4 0 3 3 9 5
9 1 5 3 6 4 6 1 1 1 4 2 6 7 8 8 6 1
0 5 9 3 4 5 0 1 5 8 3 1 9 6 1 2 9 2
1 3 9 4 5 8 4 9 2 7 7 8 4 4 4 5 3 2
2 7 6 8 7 5 0 9 5 2 4 7 5 6 5 8 1 4
7 0 5 1 1 6 5 7 8 3 7 3 7 0 9 0 7 5
4 4 6 3 4 6 4 6 2 3 1 3 7 7 4 3 7 9
2 6 0 9 3 8 3 5 1 2 9 1 8 0 5 7 1 9
7 6 5 1 2 4 2 8 2 8 4 0 2 0 5 4 7 1
7 8 1 8 2 8 2 8 2 9 9 2 3 0 7 0 5 3
7 8 6 5 3 2 2 9 8 8 9 5 8 4 6 1 0 1
```

Mark and count: 13

```
77 62 19 99 77 34 34 36 45 13 27 77
18 49 18 56 84 34 85 18 33 17 15 11
59 57 77 46 26 71 33 53 90 22 68 13
24 80 36 59 49 15 13 29 99 66 22 25
90 78 25 88 83 33 43 50 49 66 27 25
13 48 61 78 85 65 64 39 59 51 99 53
25 25 13 80 48 14 37 82 17 32 75 84
23 10 88 51 32 30 65 94 61 38 74 13
55 15 13 64 66 29 13 47 79 85 36 93
13 14 62 41 77 36 42 74 98 12 96 59
43 83 37 78 55 13 13 13 15 13 57 85
61 72 82 32 20 82 72 21 99 46 42 61
16 92 75 61 16 44 75 72 26 13 80 19
```

Are you sure? See page 195!

Now make a simple sketch of the memorized picture
with as many details as possible:

TRY TO REMEMBER!

What should you find?

- City: _____
- Name: _____
- Decrypted text: _____

day 16

WARM UP!

6 - 6 = _____	4 · 6 = _____
18 - 5 = _____	3 · 5 = _____
10 - 2 = _____	16 - 10 = _____
12 - 5 = _____	16 - 4 = _____
2 · 10 = _____	3 · 6 = _____
17 - 2 = _____	8 + 10 = _____
18 - 4 = _____	3 · 7 = _____
8 - 8 = _____	21 - 8 = _____
3 · 2 = _____	13 - 13 = _____
7 + 7 = _____	4 + 8 = _____
6 + 12 = _____	20 - 17 = _____
7 · 2 = _____	18 + 6 = _____
2 · 2 = _____	6 · 3 = _____
8 - 3 = _____	16 + 9 = _____
4 · 2 = _____	23 - 23 = _____
2 + 11 = _____	4 + 20 = _____
13 + 2 = _____	4 · 5 = _____
2 · 3 = _____	17 - 9 = _____
5 + 14 = _____	19 - 18 = _____
2 · 5 = _____	6 · 6 = _____

Decipher the following code with the "Caesar encryption".

The required character offset to the right is: 6

N B Z U _ C L M N U W I I E

_ _ _ _ _ _ _ _ _ _ _ _ _ _

Copy the decrypted text on page 197.

ABCDEFGHIJKLMNOPQRSTUVWXYZ_ABCDEF

Memorize this picture and all of its details as best as you can to make a sketch of it later.

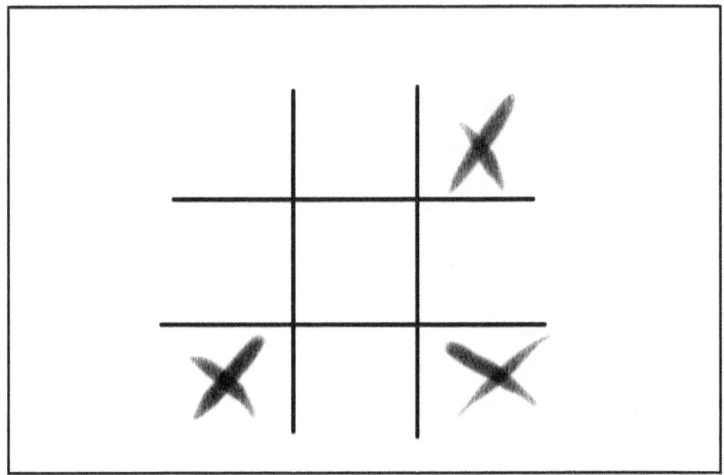

WORDS AND LETTERS

0	24
13	15
8	6
7	12
20	18
15	18
14	21
0	13
6	0
14	12
18	3
14	24
4	18
5	25
8	0
13	24
15	20
6	8
19	1
10	36

Mark and count: E

```
FEFFFFFFFFFFFFFFFFFFFFFFFFFFFFFFFFFF
FFFFFFFFFFFFFFFFFFFFFFFFFFFEFFFFFFFF
FFEFFEFFFFFFFFFFFFFFFFFFFFEFFFFFFFF
FFEFFFFFFFFFFFFFFFFFFFFFFFFFFFFFFFFF
FEFFFFFFFFEFFFFFFFFFFFFFFFFFFFFFFFFF
FFFFFFFFFFFFFFFFFFFFFFFFFFFFFFFFFFFF
EFFFFFFFEFFFFFFFFFFFFFFFFFFFFFFFFFFF
FFFFFEFFFFFFFFFFEFFFEFFFEFFFFFEFFFFF
FFFFFFFFFFEEEFFFFFFFFFFFFFFFFFFFFFFF
FFFFFFFFFFFFFFFEFEFFFFFFFFFFFFFFFFFF
FFFFFFFFFEEFFFFFFFFFFFEFFFFFFFFFFFFF
FFFFFFFFFFEFFFFFFFFFFFFFFFFFFFFFFFFF
FFFFFFFFFFFFFFFFFFFFFFFFFFFFFFFFFFFF
```

Mark and count: STOCKHOLM

```
SHOHSLTLTCOTCHSOHOLLCTHMOHOLMKLCKTL
OCOOMMOOMOSOLOTHCSTOCKHOLMOKMOHCCCO
MTTSTOCKHOLMCCLHSTOCKHOLMSSLOOHOLCS
CHCLOTHHTKOKTSTOCKHOLMCHOTSOSSLCKOC
TSLMSTOCKHOLMKOCMMOOOMOSKOMLMSOLLOO
TSTOCKHOLMCSTOCKHOLMMTMLKLMCKTTKMOO
CHOMKMSCCSTLTKOSOTLLHSKOKMOLMSMSSCO
HTLLHSLTMKSHSTOCTMSOLCCLHSTOCKHOLMO
OHMHOKOCSSSTOCKHOLMHLSTOCKHOLMOOSTK
STOCKHOLMHCCOKSTOCKHOLMHCCOSKMHHHLO
MOKCMTMCOSTOCKHOLMOTOKTOLHSOTSOMMCL
LSCOHTKHOOCKHSSMSLTCSTOCKHOLMHOHHTM
CSTOCKHOLMCOOOMCOOCCOOOOHOOSTCHTOTH
```

168

Decrypted original text from the previous page:
THE FIRST BOOK

Mark and count: AVA

```
ULDQROESCGAOGAVARBNLFTKVRUPXIARKYCB
EMDSFTEFRFGDAVAXLHZAGKWMQTJRQGCAAEK
BPPCVLJSAHXMTELGUZYIAVANJDAVAXXSCEX
MPWSAVAYXAVAZTCVLHIAVAHTBBPWQGAVADH
OJAVAOSAVAOEAIRTFAVABSJZRHHPWMHLJPH
NSVVBJFDYETPAVAXSXKVGLBTQZIXAVAZMOL
AVAVDPXHOKKOHMBGKRYFPYVMLNGTSQAVAUF
AVAICYKDXJWZUVLIGLSAVAAPVQSUAFOMQJE
DCIKQAVAOEXYGIZYJOELAROYMVMXIOPLPHC
CTLIGVBPGCCNJXOEBLKIUNONAVAPMXBGZDC
PODWIGWESLFOOUEGZLQHKCKKVTEVQGJBKXW
ZIWVODDXZLRXEZBCJGJKQTKBYRMPQHAVAUA
AUETNRJASDAVAGZNKOXJPQJGQEQZYMGVMTU
LALIAVAPRUBCLARGIKNKEOKFZIRAVALDUUH
SCAVAOHQBNOZKAHRFEEUYNGLEPTKIGZJLYP
MDUBGILIKAVAWPPKNOMAVAVUYECKVAVADSR
VMTVNLDIPLJYTMONLVRFHJMCAVAGULQSBGH
WYYKJAVARHLJZLAVAGAZXDWQNROUNPBFOTV
ZBKKGWIKLMAMYBFVCDAVAGXCHGTQRAUABZS
HNOVIBDKQNAVAZENBAPBIPITQFMSYOQMEKF
HCPPPJNEVSQVVDHYBKXFYFWYHVNBHEAVAFI
NAVAFGZZVFEJQGJSBCEQQSWUNOWNXJTZZUZ
QLZGAZWILEGMSSHBFUAVANTJXABRPSUHAVA
SZEAQFAVANSKANHNDRDHAVAAVAUJFUAVAUJ
EPJNHBLXKSKRBDGYSCIGGDSUVBAVAIVYIHV
LEKQHAVAHZHHXXXICUORVQRBDRXTTPUUGZC
IPAVAIYIIQAVALHDGAVAKGXYYCAVAJSTLWS
CRKZESIPQTSDLBWTDWYAVATDNWCROSEWLMN
SPMPNHJVRZCKCAVAAVANPRQSJYLZFURXIPG
```

15	10
25	19
21	14
53	6
7	25
30	40
49	15
56	9
40	17
6	29
14	28
25	12
20	16
23	18
48	23
40	1
31	9
20	28
59	11
38	27

Are you sure? See page 194!

CALCULATE

18	-	16	=	_____	15	+	14	=	_____

18 - 16 = _____   15 + 14 = _____

19 - 15 = _____   4 • 2 = _____

7 + 13 = _____   6 + 16 = _____

5 • 3 = _____   2 • 2 = _____

2 + 2 = _____   10 • 3 = _____

7 + 5 = _____   13 - 9 = _____

7 + 7 = _____   6 • 4 = _____

11 - 8 = _____   7 + 6 = _____

12 - 8 = _____   4 • 4 = _____

7 + 10 = _____   26 - 5 = _____

2 • 5 = _____   4 • 6 = _____

3 + 16 = _____   27 - 27 = _____

5 - 4 = _____   5 • 5 = _____

2 + 17 = _____   6 • 6 = _____

6 • 2 = _____   14 + 5 = _____

6 • 3 = _____   7 • 3 = _____

5 • 2 = _____   5 + 5 = _____

8 • 3 = _____   13 + 5 = _____

8 + 4 = _____   23 - 14 = _____

15 - 13 = _____   9 • 3 = _____

Additional tasks - only for math lovers!

3 • 5 = ____   2 • 5 = ____

13 + 12 = ____   6 + 13 = ____

3 • 7 = ____   20 - 6 = ____

21 + 32 = ____   29 - 23 = ____

49 - 42 = ____   29 - 4 = ____

3 • 10 = ____   8 • 5 = ____

27 + 22 = ____   6 + 9 = ____

8 • 7 = ____   3 • 3 = ____

45 - 5 = ____   22 - 5 = ____

2 • 3 = ____   17 + 12 = ____

7 • 2 = ____   8 + 20 = ____

6 + 19 = ____   4 • 3 = ____

42 - 22 = ____   27 - 11 = ____

43 - 20 = ____   5 + 13 = ____

6 • 8 = ____   19 + 4 = ____

46 - 6 = ____   13 - 12 = ____

39 - 8 = ____   27 - 18 = ____

10 • 2 = ____   24 + 4 = ____

31 + 28 = ____   7 + 4 = ____

15 + 23 = ____   21 + 6 = ____

FIND THE NUMBERS!

2	29
4	8
20	22
15	4
4	30
12	4
14	24
3	13
4	16
17	21
10	24
19	0
1	25
19	36
12	19
18	21
10	10
24	18
12	9
2	27

Mark and count: 6

```
3 8 0 2 8 5 1 3 9 7 3 6 5 8 4 6 2 8
4 0 1 4 1 5 1 5 5 6 6 6 0 5 7 4 4 1
5 4 7 0 0 0 5 3 1 0 1 3 3 1 5 0 9 8
0 4 1 3 1 8 3 7 7 3 3 5 2 6 7 9 8 6
5 5 2 3 7 8 0 7 4 2 3 4 4 5 0 2 5 6
6 3 2 4 3 1 3 1 0 4 0 3 2 6 0 8 4 4
6 3 1 8 7 9 2 6 4 2 3 7 4 8 5 9 0 0
3 7 9 9 3 7 4 8 5 9 3 9 4 2 8 2 0 5
9 6 6 7 2 9 9 4 0 1 1 9 0 6 9 5 5 5
0 2 7 7 4 8 6 0 2 5 3 1 5 4 3 9 3 0
4 8 7 5 1 2 1 8 5 8 0 9 9 1 2 5 8 8
1 6 1 5 4 0 4 2 6 1 7 0 5 1 2 6 0 3
0 6 6 6 3 3 7 4 9 1 7 9 5 5 6 5 2 4
```

Mark and count: 95

```
52 16 70 10 61 68 94 34 98 68 80 95
23 52 82 41 86 95 68 55 74 14 97 38
53 92 18 94 95 21 37 29 77 27 73 85
83 97 87 52 82 79 25 24 33 95 78 95
95 91 79 95 86 75 89 56 52 34 67 22
96 77 35 14 39 75 57 92 37 32 57 36
73 30 89 95 64 64 54 38 94 82 93 95
77 87 46 68 64 52 95 69 96 58 10 95
11 35 59 34 95 23 99 39 81 96 35 52
59 56 45 36 94 36 10 75 21 50 95 76
92 95 95 17 30 66 99 51 63 18 32 95
13 56 98 95 95 41 48 30 66 44 74 52
56 20 95 99 67 94 71 24 94 69 64 87
```

Are you sure? See page 195!

Now make a simple sketch of the memorized picture with as many details as possible:

TRY TO REMEMBER!

What should you find?

- City: _____
- Name: _____
- Decrypted text: _____

day 17

WARM UP!

$4 \cdot 5 =$ _____

$4 \cdot 4 =$ _____

$3 \cdot 8 =$ _____

$9 \cdot 2 =$ _____

$7 \cdot 3 =$ _____

$8 \cdot 2 =$ _____

$2 \cdot 10 =$ _____

$13 - 8 =$ _____

$7 + 3 =$ _____

$20 - 4 =$ _____

$14 - 10 =$ _____

$6 \cdot 3 =$ _____

$2 \cdot 7 =$ _____

$8 \cdot 3 =$ _____

$3 \cdot 2 =$ _____

$2 \cdot 9 =$ _____

$6 \cdot 4 =$ _____

$9 - 9 =$ _____

$10 - 9 =$ _____

$5 \cdot 4 =$ _____

$17 + 8 =$ _____

$7 \cdot 6 =$ _____

$4 + 19 =$ _____

$3 \cdot 10 =$ _____

$6 \cdot 5 =$ _____

$5 \cdot 2 =$ _____

$5 \cdot 5 =$ _____

$4 \cdot 9 =$ _____

$3 \cdot 7 =$ _____

$8 + 6 =$ _____

$3 \cdot 9 =$ _____

$10 \cdot 4 =$ _____

$9 - 8 =$ _____

$29 - 17 =$ _____

$5 + 18 =$ _____

$7 \cdot 5 =$ _____

$4 \cdot 8 =$ _____

$19 - 13 =$ _____

$17 - 10 =$ _____

$22 - 3 =$ _____

Decipher the following code with the "Caesar encryption".

The required character offset to the right is: 2

Z L B Y L M U

— — — — — — —

Copy the decrypted text on page 197.

ABCDEFGHIJKLMNOPQRSTUVWXYZ_ABCDEF

Memorize this picture and all of its details as best as you can to make a sketch of it later.

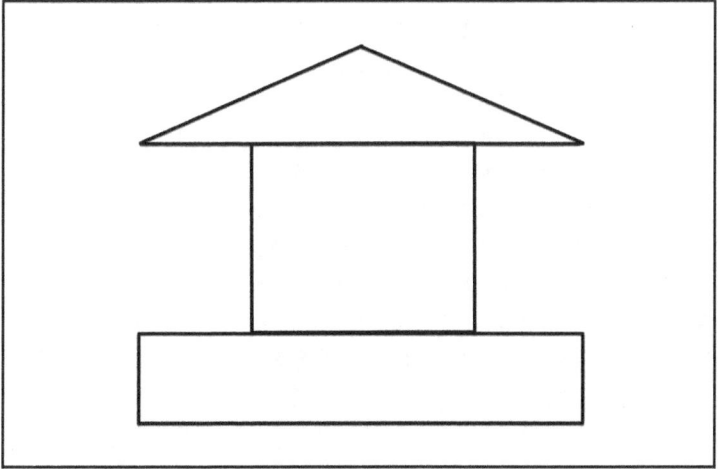

20 25

16 42

24 23

18 30

21 30

16 10

20 25

5 36

10 21

16 14

4 27

18 40

14 1

24 12

6 23

18 35

24 32

0 6

1 7

20 19

Mark and count: D

```
DBBBBBBBBBBBBBBBBBBBBBBBBBBBBBBBBBBBBBB
BBBBDBBBBBBBBBBBBBBBBBBBBBBBBBBBBBBBBBB
DBBBBBBBBBBBBBBBBBBBBBBBBBBBBBBBDBBBBB
BBBBBBBBBBBBBBBBBBBBDBBBBBBBBBBBBBBBBBB
BBBBBBBBBBBBBBBBBBBBBBBBBBBBBBBBBBBBBBB
BBBBBBBBBBBBBBBBBBBBBBBBBBBBBBBBBBBBBBB
DBBBBBBBBBBBBBBBBBBBBBBBBBBBBBBBBBBBBBB
BBBBBBBBBBBBBBBBBBBBBBBBBBBBBBBBBBBBBDB
BBBBBBBBBDBBBBBBBBBBBBBBBBBBBBBBBBDBBBB
BBBBBBBBBBBBBBBBBBBBBBBBBBBBBDBBBBBBBBB
BBBBBBBBBBDBBBBBBBBBBBBBBBBBBBBBBBBDBBB
BBBDBBBBDBBBBBBBBBBBBBBDBBBBBDBBBBDBBBB
BBBBBBBBBBBBBBBBBBBBBBBBBBBBDBBBBBBBBBB
```

Mark and count: SANTIAGO

```
NOSSAAOISNSANTIAGONOITTONNGIGNOTISA
SANTIAGOSNSASANTIAGOTOAGSNSANTIAGOO
OIOOAIAGIITAAASAATSANTIAGOSGSNOTSSA
TIIGINAAANANOSAGNATTGSAAGAOGSANNGNA
ASGSTTTGIGAINIATISISISSSOAASAASATNA
AAAOOANTAGASANTIAGOAGSNAAGITTTIGSTA
GASGOASGSAIAAIAOSNTOSANTIAGOTSINGAT
TNAOANNSANTIAGONOTOITOIGAONSGOSIANN
ASTOATAINNSANTIAGOTSNGANSANTIAGOGIN
AIATASANTIAGOSANTIAGOIASOAAAGNAAGAO
TASAGSSANTIAGOAONIATSANTIAGOIOSAASN
ASTAIGGAOSANTIAGOAATSANTIAGOATAASNT
AATIANANNTONNAAIGNATSSOIAIAAIAONTSA
```

178

Decrypted original text from the previous page:
AND NOW

Mark and count: ETHAN

```
LTETHANXIETHANYHGJMFYOETHANPETHANEX
SYHLKSPCOASIXCXTYDZCNNXMXYUVAZYJQAU
WJCZULLUPXWLOYOLAHOTZITOIOOFUBOQTVQ
XTNNIGCGPHEOEYQVIOJANQTTEUZKYBBSUFO
TETHANNTANCWGMAWXSWQETHANCETHANWYNI
BYIAANRYTGGXETHANSKVWCKCLLPTJVZMFRI
UGWYGBRATFVAQGYSZSDXDJRWVETHANUJXIQ
SFCXBATEETHANODKNSUFWRAETHANPRQJVBL
SZASNUGNXSETHANXTEJDMJZOIZFJEHYBNXH
SHWBKDUPCKBJXPYRESWBEFLETHANETHANIC
PQRSEPWLFAYNQMCHLPICIPMEBCIZWEJVYYK
TNIGQMCETHANYPNIFYLPZEIHRNZCEETHANM
ETHANWAGMJETHANUWQSMFXVHVCMHENPDHCQ
XQJEADYRZXBWBEZIAMTJCUETHANYNZSBCSQ
JWVETHANAZDNPXRXBZBMNRUCNJYJBLBUYUH
RUTEENETHANEAQJOOPHWQEWUTUDUFVYDRIX
IETHANBEHWYSJKZATOETHANMNDKWHVUNZNH
ETHANDGEEFPOVVKOWLDDIARNNXZPRXFOUCF
TGPXJEFMZMOISTEWAOETHANQGGGQOQZEAEB
RFADFVWZLCZQCRGUIJTTMAERFNDGCILFFOJ
ETHANXETHANZMEWYMGMNFUZIRVAAQKUVMMQ
OTABAWHFBAFETHANETHANBAMEDJHETHANWG
WIJJSSTKMHOBVETHANETHANOXSRPGUEQVXX
WJGXIIQNNGETHANUWEYUETHANNXTFELNRIK
QUYTESTZBOKBLBLETHANAETHANYJJXETHAN
HETHANQFFETHANGFBCXUHQKYLGJUETHANVF
MIGWRBCUVELPAIPMCZCOTSFVXDOIRLCYFZV
NBARQBAAKETHANXAXZQEUODFZUKLTGFJPIA
PSLSJXZTDGQXMJETHANWAQMVKXHOLUPEGDT
```

3	17
44	10
14	40
25	15
41	15
21	1
3	7
24	24
72	16
34	14
60	25
19	8
31	20
8	23
35	20
45	20
7	0
0	26
5	36
40	42

Are you sure? See page 194!

CALCULATE

16 - 4 = _____	4 • 7 = _____
3 • 5 = _____	19 - 12 = _____
4 • 2 = _____	8 • 3 = _____
14 - 14 = _____	13 + 4 = _____
13 + 2 = _____	8 - 7 = _____
3 • 7 = _____	30 - 7 = _____
4 + 9 = _____	8 • 2 = _____
17 - 6 = _____	7 + 17 = _____
6 + 9 = _____	5 • 2 = _____
7 + 10 = _____	7 + 11 = _____
16 + 4 = _____	26 - 10 = _____
9 • 2 = _____	13 + 11 = _____
9 + 5 = _____	25 - 4 = _____
2 + 17 = _____	9 + 21 = _____
18 - 15 = _____	15 + 8 = _____
2 • 10 = _____	30 - 5 = _____
10 + 4 = _____	3 • 3 = _____
2 • 2 = _____	24 + 4 = _____
10 + 3 = _____	15 + 14 = _____
2 • 3 = _____	18 + 4 = _____

Additional tasks - only for math lovers!

49 - 46 = _____   5 + 12 = _____

31 + 13 = _____   30 - 20 = _____

46 - 32 = _____   10 • 4 = _____

44 - 19 = _____   23 - 8 = _____

34 + 7 = _____   9 + 6 = _____

47 - 26 = _____   19 - 18 = _____

11 - 8 = _____   23 - 16 = _____

6 • 4 = _____   16 + 8 = _____

9 • 8 = _____   20 - 4 = _____

9 + 25 = _____   25 - 11 = _____

28 + 32 = _____   20 + 5 = _____

27 - 8 = _____   19 - 11 = _____

16 + 15 = _____   5 • 4 = _____

2 • 4 = _____   6 + 17 = _____

25 + 10 = _____   6 + 14 = _____

9 • 5 = _____   16 + 4 = _____

45 - 38 = _____   6 - 6 = _____

35 - 35 = _____   22 + 4 = _____

14 - 9 = _____   6 • 6 = _____

21 + 19 = _____   7 • 6 = _____

FIND THE NUMBERS!

12	28
15	7
8	24
0	17
15	1
21	23
13	16
11	24
15	10
17	18
20	16
18	24
14	21
19	30
3	23
20	25
14	9
4	28
13	29
6	22

Mark and count: 4

```
8 7 3 2 2 3 0 5 1 8 5 1 3 9 1 4 1 0
0 1 6 8 9 3 0 3 0 1 7 4 2 9 0 8 2 7
6 3 5 1 9 8 0 4 9 3 0 3 8 8 6 2 8 1
2 6 7 2 4 8 9 2 3 4 3 7 4 9 6 4 1 4
5 6 2 9 4 0 3 7 6 7 4 9 6 1 7 7 8 0
6 7 1 9 5 1 7 7 7 0 6 6 9 3 2 4 8 3
3 9 8 5 5 1 2 3 4 2 2 5 1 2 1 3 8 1
8 2 7 6 6 1 6 0 2 5 9 7 8 0 9 9 3 2
6 0 7 2 7 4 0 3 0 7 9 5 2 6 5 4 8 3
0 2 5 0 1 1 1 7 2 0 8 5 4 1 3 2 9 4
3 3 0 9 1 1 1 6 4 5 2 2 7 3 8 1 8 2
9 0 3 9 4 2 1 2 2 8 7 1 9 6 0 8 8 9
7 3 1 6 9 9 5 2 8 4 0 4 1 6 2 1 4 3
```

Mark and count: 34

```
78 45 99 66 46 79 91 48 85 34 18 60
34 21 34 39 87 26 89 63 34 17 34 19
69 78 34 37 63 44 25 72 39 85 18 98
52 22 97 77 99 63 34 15 78 74 28 89
12 61 57 67 34 23 12 34 87 76 31 79
84 17 88 39 15 35 82 18 93 93 34 27
94 25 29 62 73 27 86 24 48 15 89 34
47 42 75 16 24 66 66 11 34 60 66 73
90 99 57 12 74 40 97 40 87 63 52 19
11 69 19 30 18 85 37 54 28 26 39 27
54 70 72 89 61 15 34 18 90 37 27 72
60 36 64 34 34 28 42 17 89 58 45 42
27 44 50 30 60 15 20 30 57 28 98 60
```

Are you sure? See page 195!

Now make a simple sketch of the memorized picture
with as many details as possible:

TRY TO REMEMBER!

What should you find?

- City: _____
- Name: _____
- Decrypted text: _____

day 18

WARM UP!

8 • 3 = _____   10 + 9 = _____

5 • 2 = _____   4 • 4 = _____

19 − 15 = _____   5 • 5 = _____

3 • 4 = _____   5 + 17 = _____

3 + 5 = _____   4 + 23 = _____

10 + 8 = _____   4 • 9 = _____

5 + 15 = _____   29 − 9 = _____

15 − 11 = _____   11 − 10 = _____

3 + 13 = _____   4 • 10 = _____

11 + 7 = _____   9 + 11 = _____

2 − 2 = _____   13 + 17 = _____

9 − 2 = _____   17 + 4 = _____

8 • 2 = _____   7 • 3 = _____

16 − 9 = _____   14 + 11 = _____

3 • 8 = _____   13 − 7 = _____

3 + 10 = _____   13 − 9 = _____

20 − 6 = _____   3 • 9 = _____

10 − 10 = _____   20 + 8 = _____

19 − 9 = _____   3 • 5 = _____

6 • 3 = _____   7 • 4 = _____

Decipher the following code with the "Caesar encryption".

The required character offset to the right is: 3

B K Q B O X Q E B X K B U Q X I B S B I

_ _ _ _ _ _ _ _ _ _ _ _ _ _ _ _ _ _ _ _

Copy the decrypted text on page 197.

ABCDEFGHIJKLMNOPQRSTUVWXYZ_ABCDEF

Memorize this picture and all of its details as best as you can to make a sketch of it later.

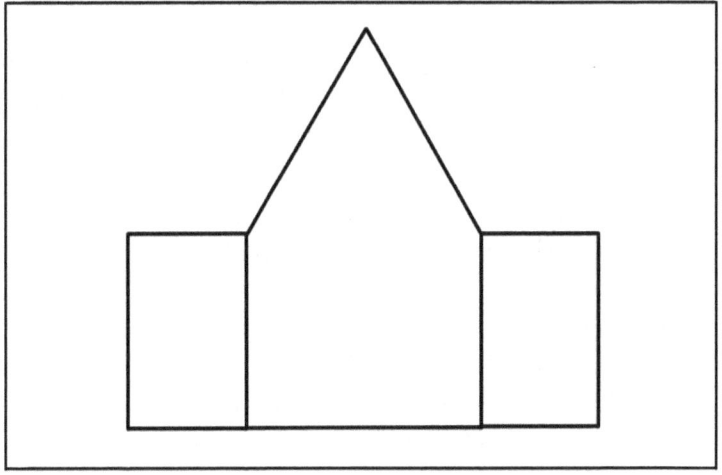

24 19

10 16

4 25

12 22

8 27

18 36

20 20

4 1

16 40

18 20

0 30

7 21

16 21

7 25

24 6

13 4

14 27

0 28

10 15

18 28

Mark and count: Q

```
OOOOOQOOOOOOOOOOOOOOOOOOOOOOOOOOOOOOO
OOOOOOOOOOOOOOOOOOOOOOOOQOOOOOOOOOOOO
OOOOOOOOOOOOOOOOOOOOOOOQOOOOOOOOOOOOO
OOOOQOOOOOOOOOOOOOOOOOOOOOOOOOOQOQOOO
QOOOOOOOOOOOOOOOOOOOOOOOOQOOOOOOOOOOO
OOOOOOOOOOOOOOOOOOOQOOOOOOOOOOOOOOOOO
QOOOOOOOOOOOOOOOOOQOOOOOOOOOOOOQOOO
OOOOOOOOOOQOOOOOQOOOOQOOOOOOOOOOOOO
OQOOOOOOOQOOOOOOOQQOOOOOOOOOOOOOOO
OOOOOOOOOOOOOOOOOOOOOOOOOOOOOOOOOOOOO
OQQOOOOOQOOOOOOOOOQOOOOOOOOOOOOOOO
OOOOOOOOOOOOOOOOOOOQOOOOOOOOOOOOOOOO
OOOOOOOOOOOOOOOOOOOOOOOOOOOOOOOOOOOOO
```

Mark and count: NASSAU

```
SSNSSNSAASNANNSSAASUSNNNAUAUSSNSASA
ANANASSAUAANSNNNASSAUSSSUSSNASAUASS
NNASSAUSAAASASSANASSAUSAAASASUSUNNN
AANSUSAASANSSNNAASAANASSAUUNSUASANU
NASSAUAAUNASSAUSAUSANNASSAUNASSAUSA
UUAASSSUAUUNAUAASUNASAUANASSAUASUSS
ANASSAUUNASSAUAUNAAAUSSNSAAAUSAASSA
ANNASSAUUAASNUNASASSASSSUUUUASSAANA
AUANSSAUSSANSUNNUUSUNSNSSNAASSUASAN
NANANASSAUAUSNUNASSAUANASSAUUNAAAAN
NASSAUUSSAASSNASSAUSUSSSANASSAUNUAN
SANUASNNAUASUANASSNASSAUNUASSAUASSU
AAASASUASSNNASSAUNNSNASSAUUAUSSSASS
```

Decrypted original text from the previous page:
ENTER THE NEXT LEVEL

Mark and count: MAX

45	30
8	17
43	15
36	15
18	15
45	36
27	20
20	27
58	30
42	30
53	14
47	14
32	30
18	20
38	24
21	30
70	26
19	18
43	8
49	48

```
XOOZJAGPPCSHJFANZVBMAXJRCCVXVWHQGIX
MMHYZLKGBSHJTMGYNMAXUMZGLYXMAXZXHBH
FDFYLXMAXFZGUNZQQUUIZFNAMAXMAXEINGP
BKBWGXMAXUOGLVZLDWLSYDFPBUEESUIMAXP
EMAXUJHSTZJMAXXYMTQEEDKTQFVGSRQMAXP
KYRBXMAXBMYYYDXMAXLUMAXJWXCYDBMAXGD
TWSERMAXYJNYMSENJWMAXCROSSZPNQRDNYC
FNSBEPXEKRCWBBIJXMAXDUUOWWMAXSIEILF
PZKVGOGWFMAXQAIFDFFTEOBUPBGMAXSEMPB
SOJEXLMAXEMBXNVWULRKKXYKQYAMAXVTCVU
KZXHNUQAAFKFPLZNQEEZXWNFVEIPUNWXHCR
CPLXZNSGIMAXMAXXEHGRJVCNSEEUYLYWBMZ
LJMICAIQUYBOSLYZBLEZYBCCWBHQKMAXYPI
MAXLHNNPZIMAXGBTMAXRIHNBHRIVZIGCMAX
JCJUZAVHDKTVCRJRRSEVNKIBMAAVEWHMAXR
SGFNELSRNLCESMGHUBOJACYHCDYCEBWTEMQ
UZCUDTTDQBRNFQAXLJUCLRBYNPSEPZWVEFE
FCMAXPSIMAXHBJLDHJQSDSWEGKDRORWTJKT
NXQLZGFRIIQLCYZOPKRFQXHSNRCTHCZMAXY
PTGCQCMAXUBWXHMAXAWDMAXPJSJCUQRKXAI
XGNMAXIYBIFEMSIJCCGDJIJXSAIGUIDTUYD
MAXPVWDTNENMNFKAQBZJOXEEURVMWMAXXAF
XWDAEDMAXONHIHFGGDYYLBJBEODQTTPEPQR
NTOJDHLJKMAXWRUMAXDCJICQSNYZSJSUUNJ
SCXIQAKRLXKEMAXAHJVNSXJFMAXDLHQOAVV
NBDUCJFZNXTNADSRSBJLYXKNSGJGEIRZNZR
QJPQQAZUISLLKCNKAWIVMAXPEGJPDAYESZJ
MAXMAXMEFMMOWMDVMAXCIQKMAXUFRMAXSSZ
BEIJMAXRNMAXHHVBUEHZGOMAXRGNQMAXAAY
```

Are you sure? See page 194!

CALCULATE

19 - 5 = ____	4 + 26 = ____
2 + 11 = ____	5 • 8 = ____
10 + 3 = ____	25 - 22 = ____
20 - 2 = ____	5 + 16 = ____
3 • 4 = ____	29 - 3 = ____
6 - 6 = ____	10 - 7 = ____
3 • 3 = ____	12 + 16 = ____
10 • 2 = ____	8 • 4 = ____
13 - 4 = ____	7 - 5 = ____
2 + 15 = ____	7 • 5 = ____
2 • 3 = ____	12 + 7 = ____
16 - 10 = ____	9 • 5 = ____
20 - 20 = ____	5 • 5 = ____
4 + 3 = ____	16 - 5 = ____
14 - 2 = ____	28 - 3 = ____
9 + 10 = ____	8 + 21 = ____
12 - 7 = ____	2 • 2 = ____
15 - 12 = ____	6 • 7 = ____
5 - 3 = ____	14 + 5 = ____
7 + 13 = ____	24 + 4 = ____

Additional tasks - only for math lovers!

$29 + 16 =$ _____　　$9 + 21 =$ _____

$4 \cdot 2 =$ _____　　$22 - 5 =$ _____

$8 + 35 =$ _____　　$3 \cdot 5 =$ _____

$4 \cdot 9 =$ _____　　$6 + 9 =$ _____

$43 - 25 =$ _____　　$29 - 14 =$ _____

$10 + 35 =$ _____　　$9 \cdot 4 =$ _____

$3 \cdot 9 =$ _____　　$10 \cdot 2 =$ _____

$5 \cdot 4 =$ _____　　$9 \cdot 3 =$ _____

$22 + 36 =$ _____　　$18 + 12 =$ _____

$7 \cdot 6 =$ _____　　$5 \cdot 6 =$ _____

$27 + 26 =$ _____　　$7 \cdot 2 =$ _____

$36 + 11 =$ _____　　$8 + 6 =$ _____

$38 - 6 =$ _____　　$21 + 9 =$ _____

$3 \cdot 6 =$ _____　　$2 \cdot 10 =$ _____

$7 + 31 =$ _____　　$7 + 17 =$ _____

$41 - 20 =$ _____　　$17 + 13 =$ _____

$10 \cdot 7 =$ _____　　$7 + 19 =$ _____

$42 - 23 =$ _____　　$5 + 13 =$ _____

$23 + 20 =$ _____　　$2 \cdot 4 =$ _____

$25 + 24 =$ _____　　$6 \cdot 8 =$ _____

FIND THE NUMBERS!

14	30
13	40
13	3
18	21
12	26
0	3
9	28
20	32
9	2
17	35
6	19
6	45
0	25
7	11
12	25
19	29
5	4
3	42
2	19
20	28

Mark and count: 9

```
2 9 0 6 6 6 5 7 5 9 7 4 0 5 6 9 9 0
1 4 1 7 5 8 4 8 3 5 6 4 6 7 4 3 4 6
3 9 7 8 0 1 6 3 6 4 1 6 7 3 1 8 6 7
7 6 4 9 8 4 0 0 9 5 6 9 1 0 3 6 0 0
0 0 1 0 6 2 9 7 1 8 0 6 3 8 6 2 3 0
5 1 1 6 1 8 3 5 1 0 1 9 1 4 8 4 7 9
0 5 1 0 5 6 6 3 6 4 5 5 3 0 1 7 5 1
2 6 3 4 7 0 4 5 1 9 9 8 4 5 9 5 6 9
9 2 9 5 7 6 3 4 4 4 0 9 0 7 0 5 9 8
9 6 0 2 3 8 3 7 2 6 3 5 2 9 7 9 1 9
0 0 1 7 7 9 9 4 8 9 8 5 1 7 5 6 1 3
7 2 2 2 8 4 1 4 0 5 0 9 7 2 4 0 7 2
9 6 2 1 9 3 0 0 1 0 6 5 5 5 8 3 1 9
```

Mark and count: 72

```
94 37 31 89 36 92 92 28 99 19 72 38
95 30 95 54 37 35 85 44 26 34 26 44
62 20 36 55 72 72 65 85 28 83 40 52
22 28 11 13 95 94 13 68 22 77 66 21
22 33 39 83 17 51 90 84 46 86 59 68
95 81 59 97 50 99 52 73 90 76 48 68
24 72 13 81 94 89 89 69 19 73 49 39
24 48 96 87 44 44 18 58 28 62 14 41
53 39 17 93 89 50 68 81 86 30 72 15
40 75 19 70 82 84 30 29 76 63 85 39
95 99 25 15 11 38 10 43 97 46 72 65
90 72 55 99 72 72 13 97 52 38 41 34
16 22 41 31 59 89 34 72 64 33 68 40
```

Are you sure? See page 195!

Now make a simple sketch of the memorized picture
with as many details as possible:

TRY TO REMEMBER!

What should you find?

- City: _____
- Name: _____
- Decrypted text: _____

RESULTS - WORDS AND LETTERS

page		number	page		number
18	a	22	108	a	21
18	b	16	108	b	16
19		43	109		46
28	a	14	118	a	19
28	b	15	118	b	31
29		36	119		51
38	a	19	128	a	27
38	b	20	128	b	16
39		46	129		38
48	a	34	138	a	18
48	b	23	138	b	18
49		46	139		49
58	a	21	148	a	22
58	b	24	148	b	18
59		41	149		45
68	a	18	158	a	22
68	b	17	158	b	17
69		36	159		54
78	a	18	168	a	24
78	b	15	168	b	15
79		37	169		49
88	a	19	178	a	18
88	b	21	178	b	16
89		43	179		42
98	a	24	188	a	24
98	b	23	188	b	22
99		33	189		55

RESULTS - FIND THE NUMBERS

page	number		page	number
22 a	23		112 a	20
22 b	14		112 b	11
32 a	21		122 a	24
32 b	15		122 b	17
42 a	17		132 a	24
42 b	22		132 b	25
52 a	26		142 a	20
52 b	15		142 b	25
62 a	19		152 a	23
62 b	17		152 b	16
72 a	16		162 a	25
72 b	14		162 b	14
82 a	24		172 a	23
82 b	18		172 b	19
92 a	29		182 a	21
92 b	14		182 b	15
102 a	23		192 a	30
102 b	12		192 b	10

ALWAYS REMEMBER:
YOU ARE NOT A COMPUTER!

Have fun - not frustration!

In order to train your brain, just find as much as you can as quickly as possible. If you have found around 90%, you are already very good!

ARE YOU
CURIOUS ABOUT
WHAT YOU FOUND OUT?

HERE YOU CAN WRITE DOWN
THE DECODED TEXT
FOR EACH UNIT!

DECRYPTED CODE

(1)_____ _____ (2)_____

_____ (3)_____ _____

(4)_____ _____ (5)_____

_____ (6)_____

(7)_____ •

(8)_____ ´ _____ _____ _____

(9)_____ _____ (10)_____

_____ (11)_____ _____

_____ _____ (12)_____ _____

(13)_____ _____ **!**

(14)_____ _____ **!**

(15)_____ _____ (16)_____ _____

_____ • (17)_____ _____ **:**

(18)_____ _____

_____ _____ **!**

BOOKS OF THE SERIES

www.alexanderhalm.de

SPACE FOR YOUR NOTES